C000212752

"I have known Rabbi Bernice W[eiss] [for] years and can attest that she is a te[acher who] inculcates in her students her pass[ion for] culture, and history and, above all, [contem]porary life. Rabbi Weiss has the gi[ft] [to explain the] complex and varied challenges involved on the journey that Jews-by-choice undertake. In her work with her students, she integrates mind and heart—recognizing the uniqueness of each individual and offering the mosaic of Judaism as an opportunity for meaning, joy, and personal growth. Rabbi Weiss is one of our Jewish community's treasures, and her book reflects both her philosophy and her talent."

—Rabbi Jonathan A. Schnitzer
Senior Rabbi B'nai Israel Congregation
Rockville, Maryland

"In our contemporary world of autonomy and choice, stories of individuals who find themselves walking new spiritual paths can be unusual and compelling. Rabbi Weiss is a spiritual guide par excellence for these seekers of the way. Whether the individuals come from strong attachment to ritual and family traditions or whether they come from a place of philosophic inquiry, the men and women of all ages whose stories unfold on these pages are a fascinating reflection of the modern spiritual condition. These accounts will be moving to any reader, whether they are confirmed in their faith, looking for answers to eternal questions, or looking for permission to live in the tension of certainty and uncertainty that can be part of a mature faith."

—Rabbi Gerald Serotta
Executive Director of the InferFaith
Conference of Metropolitan Washington
Washington, DC

"I am honored to have worked with Rabbi Weiss over the years as she has brought countless students under the arms of the Devine Presence and into the arms of the Jewish people. Rabbi Weiss imparts a love of Judaism and a sense of belonging and responsibility towards the Jewish people and Israel. Her impressive students have accepted important roles in our congregation and we have all been enriched by their enthusiasm and commitment. We are all fortunate that Rabbi Weiss has chosen to share their stories."

—Rabbi Michael Safra
B'nai Israel Congregation
Rockville, Maryland

"Working together with Rabbi Weiss is an opportunity to realize how lucky her students are to have the chance to study with her. Her book provides unique insight into the sacred journey toward becoming Jewish. Students who interact with Rabbi Weiss are learning from not only a gifted teacher, but a caring friend. My hope is that the students who learn with her will continue to have the opportunity to interact with many caring and loving members of our people. In her book, Rabbi Weiss provides a special guide to its readers in what being Jewish can mean to all of us."

—Rabbi Bruce Aft
Congregation Adat Reyim
Springfield, VA

"I had the privilege and joy to study with Rabbi Bernice K. Weiss, an amazing Jewish woman and trailblazer in every sense who has changed the lives of hundreds of people. With her inspiring teaching of Judaism, her warm personality, her infinite tolerance, and patience, Rabbi Weiss helped me discover spiritual meaning in everyday life and find a renewed sense of purpose in our chaotic world."

—Anne Dronnier-Kaufmann

"Rabbi Bernice Weiss is an exceptional Rabbi who has assisted hundreds of persons through the path of conversion to Judaism. Rabbi Weiss has years of experience in the conversion process to Judaism. The conversion process can take up to a year or greater. Judaism is a religion of intellect, of deep biblical history, of Jewish customs, of biblical laws, and of spiritual significance for every Jew. The path of conversion is of deep, personal, and individual choice. Rabbi Weiss ties together all of these elements in the path of conversion which unlocks that deep, personal choice to become Jewish.

"The path to conversion with Rabbi Weiss led me to further recover the roots of Judaism of my Sephardim ancestors from that part of the ancient world, the region of Spain. The path has led me to discover and continue the search of that fascinating history of the Jews in Spain, which I now comprehend much better after becoming Jewish. The impact of becoming Jewish has been of great personal and spiritual significance. It was made possible by Rabbi Weiss. In a few short words, I express my deep gratitude."

—Arturo Castro, Esq

"Rabbi Bernice Weiss is an exceptional, inspiring teacher, guiding her students through the life-changing process of conversion with deep intellect and a warm heart. Her love of Judaism and passion for study and teaching, are palpable. My studies under her left me with not only substantial knowledge of Judaism, but also the thirst to learn more, as well as the confidence to find my own unique place in the Jewish community. Conversion is an extremely personal journey, which at times can make one feel vulnerable. With her sensitive wit, Rabbi Weiss is the best guide that I could have ever hoped to find to lead me on my own path of becoming Jewish."

—Venla Sipila, PhD

"It can be very intimidating entering a synagogue and feeling everyone there knows more about the religion then you do. With Rabbi Weiss, you not only get a teacher but a friend. She is welcoming and sets an environment where you are comfortable asking questions and wanting to learn more. She played a pivotal role in my conversion process, giving me the opportunity to not only grow spiritually but gained a sense of belonging with the Jewish people."

—Andrew Ginn

"The initial idea of changing religions is intimidating for reasons such as, 'Will they except me?', 'Am I ready to change my outlook on life, future partners?', and 'Do I fully even understand the journey I am about to embark?'. It took me a few years to even put into words what I had been feeling about the Jewish faith and how I desperately wanted to be a part of it's belief system, culture, and family values. In essence, I didn't have to change my thought process at all; instead, I cultivated the feelings and emotions I had already been feeling into a way of life. I find what Rabbi Weiss calls, 'Living Life for Life's Sake' to be one of the essential pillars of the study of Judaism.

"I truly believe that my path to find Judaism would have been a completely different experience if I had not met Rabbi Weiss. She has opened up my heart and mind to the true beauty of the faith, the struggle of generations past and how to be a proud member of the community moving forward. My faith in general in a higher power has become strengthened from my time meeting with Rabbi, and I constantly feel challenged in a spiritually positive way during our weekly meetings. She is a godsend and a powerful teacher, leader, and mentor, to say the very least. Thank you from the bottom of my heart."

—Katie Shannon

"I am so grateful to have met and learned from Rabbi Weiss. She is a patient, wonderful, caring, kind, respectful, intelligent, and compassionate person. Her commitment and enthusiasm for Judaism is apparent. I am grateful for all that she did for me during my conversion process. The entire process was an amazing experience. Indeed, it was one of the best journeys of my life. I am grateful for her weekly one-on-one work with me. Throughout the conversion process, I learned so much about Judaism, life, and myself, and reached a spiritual goal. Thank you to Rabbi Weiss for assisting me to find the peace and comfort that is associated with being Jewish and living a Jewish life."

—Nat (Noah) Rasmussen, PhD

"Rabbi Weiss has shepherded many students interested in learning about Jewish faith, history, and culture—generally (though not always) in preparation for conversion before marriage. I count myself lucky to be one of her students and have benefited greatly from this learned teacher. I have enjoyed our tutoring sessions, and I consider the rabbi a friend.

"The rabbi's instructions are intellectually stimulating in the best tradition of the rabbinical dialectic over the centuries, yet they're also accessible, helpful, practical guides to becoming Jewish. She not only welcomes all questions, and questioning in general, and encourages her students to develop faith that is true to the Torah but she also accommodates doubt and is at home in her students' daily lives. The end result is a full understanding not just of Judaism but of how to be Jewish, in a way that is a source of great strength to her students.

"Rabbi Weiss is a wonderful ambassador of the Jewish faith and culture, and I glad that I have had her as a teacher."

—Samuel B. Russell, Esq.

The Secrets
of Becoming
Jewish

Rabbi Bernice K. Weiss
with Nancy Kirsch

The Washington Institute
for Conversion and the Study of Judaism

Library of Congress Cataloging-in-Publication Data is available through the Library of Congress

ISBN-13: 978-0-6923-9606-3 (trade paper)
ISBN-10: 0-6923-9606-3 (trade paper)

Publisher: The Washington Institute for
Conversion and the Study of Judaism
P.O. Box 342105
West Bethesda, Maryland 20827

Cover design by CreateSpace
Interior design and formatting by Tonya Woodworth

To the Past
My father and mother,
Hyman and Lucille Kimel

To the Future
My children,
Rachael, Jonathan, and Stephanie,
and my grandchildren,
Chloe Gabrielle and Sydney Maya

CONTENTS

FOREWORD

Rabbi Bernice K. Weiss's exceptionally moving book *The Secrets of Becoming Jewish* comes just at the right time. The October 21, 2013, Pew Research Center Survey of American Jews—the first such survey ever done by a non-sectarian organization—was a wake-up call for the American Jewish leadership but not to Rabbi Weiss. It did contain some positive news: there were more American Jews—6.7 million—than the population reported on most previous surveys by Jewish institutions (around 5.2 to 5.5 million) and that the majority of American Jews were "proud to be Jewish and have a strong sense of belonging to the Jewish people."

However, the survey revealed concerning news as well: The general US population is growing at a faster rate than the population of American Jews, whose birth rates are fairly stagnant. In addition, the percentage of American adults who identify themselves as Jewish by religion is less than 2 percent of the entire population. Some 78 percent of American Jewish adults identify themselves as "Jews by religion" and 22 percent as "Jews of no religion." They identify themselves as Jewish simply on the basis of ancestry, ethnicity, or culture. In contrast, for the youngest adult generation of Jews, the so-called

Millennials, the corresponding percentages are 68 percent and 32 percent; nearly one in three young Jewish adults self-identity as "Jews of no religion."

But most disturbing—and most relevant to Rabbi Weiss's remarkable work, which she captures so beautifully in this book—is the intermarriage rate, which has increased dramatically in the last several decades. Of the Jewish survey respondents who have married since 2000, nearly 60 percent have a non-Jewish spouse. In contrast, of those who married in the 1980s, approximately 40 percent married a non-Jewish spouse. Before 1970, only 17 percent of such marriages were interfaith! While this represents a welcome assimilation of American Jews into the mainstream of American life, a reduction in anti-Semitism in the United States, and general acceptance of Jews in our country, the consequences have serious implications for Jewish continuity. At the very same time, the general American public embraces Jews in every aspect of American society. As a result, many Jews are marrying outside their religion and, more often than not, their spouses do not convert to Judaism. Of intermarried Jews whose spouses choose not to convert, 80 percent of them are not raising their children in the Jewish religion and all of them are less likely (than couples where both spouses are Jewish, either by birth or conversion) to participate in Jewish communal activities, belong to Jewish institutions, or feel an attachment to the State of Israel.

There are many ways to attempt to deal with this challenge, including creating experiences for young Jews to visit Israel through the Taglit-Birthright program, developing stronger Jewish educational programs for all ages, accepting intermarried couples into Jewish institutions, and performing Jewish weddings for intermarrying couples who pledge to raise their children in the Jewish religion. Through these initiatives, we can hope to inculcate all such individuals with the beauty of Judaism in all its manifestations, be they religious, cultural, artistic, political, or spiritual.

The most often ignored antidote is conversion to Judaism for the non-Jewish spouse or spouse-to-be. Conversions are certainly possible and have been throughout the five thousand-plus-year history of Jews. But even today, conversions can be difficult and are fraught with hurdles; rabbis don't actively encourage conversions, as proselytizing is not consistent with Jewish tenets. Today, only some 10 percent of non-Jewish spouses convert to Judaism.

Decades ago, however, Rabbi Bernice Weiss decided to try, perhaps single-handedly, to change this paradigm of conversion. After she put aside her profitable business selling *Judaica* (jewlery, art, textiles, etc. from Israel), she enrolled as a mid-life adult in rabbinical school. For more than twenty years, she has devoted herself to working with adults who wish to convert. Some of her students seek her out because they have fallen in love with someone of the Jewish faith; others simply feel an abiding connection to Judaism. Through a yearlong course of study, where students meet weekly with Rabbi Weiss, students learn about Judaism's laws and tenets, history, language, customs, and mores.

Rabbi Weiss has adapted her program to the realities of the twenty-first century mobile society. Many study with her in person, adjusting their work and family commitments; others learn long-distance via Skype. During her more than two decades of work, she has tutored more than four hundred students. They flock to her because of her passion and love of Judaism, her warmth and caring, and her ability to convey the best of our traditions in ways to engage her students.

Her book is important because she combines intermarriage statistics with case studies on couples and individuals with whom she has worked, including a Muslim man who grew up in Lebanon, a young gay man who found the warmth and support that he lacked in his Pentecostal Christian upbringing, and a Texas physician—in an interfaith marriage—whose commitment to Judaism is so strong that two of her three children have converted. These are just a handful of the stories you will read in this book; each story reveals the relationships between Rabbi Weiss and her students, the challenges they face, and how she helps them overcome barriers to conversion.

No one person, not even someone like Rabbi Weiss—with all the energy and dedication that she possesses—can individually alter the state of Jewish life in America, as reported in the Pew Research Center survey. But *The Secrets of Becoming Jewish* should be an inspiration for more rabbis to become proactive in conversion, to recognize that religiously mixed marriages are a reality, and to do everything possible to bring these intermar-

ried couples into the Jewish fold while encouraging the
non-Jewish spouse to consider conversion to the world's
oldest continuous religion.

—Ambasssador Stuart E. Eizenstat
Chief White House Domestic Policy Adviser
to President Carter; US Ambassador to
the EuropeanUnion, Under Secretary of
Commerce, Under Secretary of State, and
Deputy Secretary of Treasury; and
Special Adviser to the President
on Holocaust Issues in the
Clinton Administration

ACKNOWLEDGEMENTS

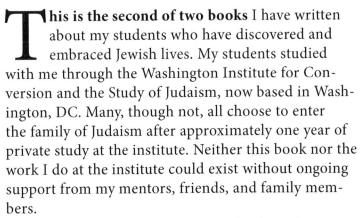

This is the second of two books I have written about my students who have discovered and embraced Jewish lives. My students studied with me through the Washington Institute for Conversion and the Study of Judaism, now based in Washington, DC. Many, though not, all choose to enter the family of Judaism after approximately one year of private study at the institute. Neither this book nor the work I do at the institute could exist without ongoing support from my mentors, friends, and family members.

I am grateful to the rabbis who helped me along my own journey. Their pluralistic approaches reflect my method of teaching, and I consider myself fortunate to work with rabbis from all Jewish movements. I want to say a special thank you to Rabbi Matthew Simon—rabbi emeritus of B'nai Israel Congregation in Rockville, Maryland—who encouraged me throughout my entire rabbinical career to follow my life's work. I also thank Rabbis Jonathan Schnitzer and Michael Safra of B'nai Israel Congregation in Rockville, Maryland; they, too, have stood by me and believed in me throughout the years.

I could not do what I do without the help of Rabbi Bruce Aft of Congregation Adat Reyim (A Community of Friends) in Springfield, Virginia, and Rabbi Gerry Se-rotta of Congregation Shirat Hanefesh (Song of the Soul) in Chevy Chase, Maryland, who have contributed their time and expertise to sit on a *beit din* (rabbinical court of Jewish laws) and help bring potential converts into Judaism to complete their journeys. I am eternally grateful to both of them.

I would be lost without my students, a rabbi without a purpose. They are insightful and inquisitive, perceptive and philosophical. Although they come as strangers, they become dear friends, even before they complete their studies. Their presence enriches my own practice of Judaism.

I owe a special thanks to three individuals, including two gifted women who helped bring this project to fruition. First, I thank my dear friend Stuart Eizenstat, a former US ambassador to the European Union and former US deputy secretary of the treasury. Despite his professional and career commitments, he has consistently and generously shared with me his wisdom and vast breadth of knowledge. He is a true friend, one who has offered me enduring kindnesses throughout the many years of our friendship.

Timothea Howard, one of my former students, interviewed many of the individuals whose stories appear in these chapters. Her love of Judaism enabled her to ask her fellow converts insightful and thoughtful questions.

A special thanks to Sheryl Silverman—contributing author of *Converting to Judaism*—who helped me develop the title for this book, which has now become a reality.

I owe a huge thanks and appreciation to Oded Harari. He has been my strength and faithful supporter, standing by my side, for many years. I could not have done this sacred work without his encouragement and and steadfast guidance.

I also want to thank Tonya Woodworth for her extraordinary editorial skills and astute understanding of the publishing world. Without her, this book would not be in the readers hands.

Last but not least, I thank my co-author for this book, Nancy Kirsch. Although we did not know one another when we began this project, she quickly became my invaluable partner on this journey. Her insight into the students' spoken and unspoken words enabled us to assemble their provocative and poignant stories, which come to life on these pages. This book would not exist without her expertise and assistance.

INTRODUCTION
The Secrets of Becoming Jewish

I was raised in a household filled with Jewish love, life, and laughter. My paternal grandfather was an Orthodox rabbi and *hazzan* (cantor); my father was director of the Zionist Organization of America for more than forty years. During those years, I lived among people who knew and understood, relished and appreciated our Jewish traditions, rituals, prayers, and beliefs. Those childhood experiences shaped me to be who I am today and led me to become a rabbi.

Shortly after the Conservative movement allowed the ordination of women as rabbis in 1985, I entered rabbinical school, leaving a successful career as a co-owner of a beautiful shop selling *Judaica* (jewlery, art, textiles, etc. from Israel). Even as a merchant, I surrounded myself with "all things Jewish." When I became a rabbi, I fell in love with teaching people about Judaism. It's fitting that I found that calling, for the word "rabbi" simply means "teacher."

Since 1991, when I founded the Washington Institute for Conversion and the Study of Judaism, a 501(c)(3) nonprofit organization, I have been teaching students who generally come to me through referrals and recommendations or after they themselves complete my course titled Basic Judaism for Jews and Non-Jews Alike. At the conclusion of that seven-week class, in which we discuss, study, read, and learn from the Torah as well as many modern texts, many of my students continue one-on-one study sessions with me to study Judaism in more depth, with the possibility of converting to Judaism. Some have fallen in love with a Jewish partner or future spouse and want to share that partner's religion while others were attracted to Judaism's strong foundation in social justice. Still others find Judaism's intellectual rigor enticing and intriguing. Other students who consider conversion find me through referrals or recommendations from other rabbis and my former students.

Some believe that Judaism, now more than 5,700 years old, is facing a crisis in America. According to "A Portrait of Jewish Americans," an October 1, 2013, publication of the Pew Research Center's Religion & Public Life Project (The Pew Project), 58 percent of American Jews who have married since 2000 married non-Jewish spouses; in contrast, only 17 percent of American Jews who married before 1970 married non-Jews.

The Pew Research Center, a nonpartisan think tank that conducts demographic research, is part of the Pew Charitable Trusts. The center does not take policy positions. The Pew Project reports that Jews have the highest intermarriage (marrying outside one's religion) of all religious groups in the United States; Mormons have the lowest, followed by Muslims. In addition to our high intermarriage rate, approximately one-half of all American

Jewish adults are currently unmarried. Of these, some never married, others are widowed or divorced.

The American Jewish population of 6.7 million offers a good news/bad news narrative: It's positive because our numbers are increasing, not falling, but it's disheartening that the Jewish population, according to the Pew Project, is growing at a slower rate than the overall population in the United States. Given these facts—high intermarriage rate, significant number of unmarried Jews, and the miniscule percentage Jews represent of the US population—this book's messages are invaluable. And, given these facts, it's clear that it is, indeed, a perilous time for many Jewish communities across the United States. While most Jewish movements neither proselytize nor solicit conversions, individuals of all ages and backgrounds who wish to study and learn about Judaism in an intimate setting have the opportunity to do so. After approximately a year of study, students who choose to convert to Judaism are able to do so. Students who simply want to expand their knowledge and understanding of Judaism to better understand their Jewish partner or spouse benefit from their study.

Each student brings his or her unique and fresh perspective to the study experience, which often requires significant commitments in both time and energy. My students are remarkable; many rearrange work schedules and juggle family commitments to study with me in person while others study and learn via Skype.

I am constantly grateful for the opportunities to introduce yet another student to Judaism's history, texts, religious practices, language, and mores. Having taught hundreds of students in my class, Basic Judaism for Jews and Non-Jews Alike, and more than 400 prospective conversion students during the past twenty-plus years, I am enriched and enlightened by their queries and their comments. As they embrace Judaism, the religion and culture I love so dearly, I am inspired. Whether I perform the marriage of a couple who studied with me, attend their baby naming, or simply reconnect with them at *Shabbat* (the Jewish Sabbath) dinners, I am awed by these students' passion for and love of Judaism, a passion and love that I hope to share with others.

I was blessed to have been born a Jew, I am blessed by my students' commitment and passion to learn and study, and I continue to be blessed to share my knowledge of and love of Judaism with my students.

CHAPTER 1

From Beirut to Washington, DC From Islam to Judaism

An Anti-Jewish Homeland Doesn't Deter Embracing Judaism

All my students' stories are rich with emotion and meaning, but Nour and Reda's story is especially noteworthy: The couple, both Muslim, grew up in Lebanon, a nation inculcated with strong anti-Jewish, anti-Israel beliefs and attitudes. After college, they met through mutual friends and fell in love.

Reda, whose parents died when he was on the cusp

of adulthood, studied the history of Judaism, Islam, and Christianity from an early age. Although it was nearly impossible to find neutral or positive writings on Judaism, Reda's reading and studying led him to reject Islam and Christianity. With that, he turned toward Judaism—something wholly unheard of in his native country. A job offer for Nour, Reda's wife of nine years, brought them from Lebanon to the Washington, DC, area. When Reda contacted me only a few days after they had moved to the United States, he expressed some fears that I might think him a terrorist.

Studying with Reda and getting to know both Reda and Nour has been a remarkable gift to me. The couple, who both work in the Washington, DC, area—he for a nonprofit organization and she for a nongovernmental organization—is passionate about both learning more and fully participating in the Jewish community. At the time I write this essay, Reda was still in the process of studying for his conversion.

Although she is not currently pursuing converting to Judaism, Nour welcomes learning more about the connections between Islam and Judaism.

That Reda could risk significant legal troubles, including imprisonment, if he returned to Lebanon and identified as a Jew is heartbreaking. That Reda, with his Lebanese passport, will never be permitted to enter Israel and visit Jerusalem, a long-held dream for him, is equally sobering. Nevertheless, those truths demonstrate his commitment to the religion of Abraham, a biblical character who has long intrigued Reda.

Reda's Early Years & His Transitions

Reda: Going to Jerusalem is my highest dream. I don't know if I will ever be able to get there because of my Lebanese passport. Since Israel and Lebanon are considered to be at war with each other, citizens from one country can't visit the other.

I was born in 1973 in Beirut, Lebanon, a country filled with hatred for the Jews. Many Lebanese individuals—some Christians, some Muslims—have a political hatred for Israelis and all Jews; they don't differentiate between Israelis and other Jews. My Muslim family was fairly, but not totally, secular and generally respectful of religions. I went to Catholic school when I was a child, and my best friend was a Christian. As a child, I had no interactions with Jewish people; my parents' one Jewish friend left Lebanon in the late 1960s or early 1970s because of pressure on the Jews.

As a curious child, I wanted to know more about religion, God, and history. When my parents bought me a set of books based on the Koran, I started learning about prophets or, as Islam calls them, messengers.

At first, I started studying the historical aspects of Islam and Christianity; but in my teenage years, I struggled to find materials to read about Judaism. In the Arab world, it was almost impossible to find anything written objectively about Jews. I could find plenty of writings against Jews written by Muslim or Christian Arabs. As I was growing more mature and reading more, I started to question things that I'd learned. I was always uncomfortable with Christmas's commercial elements and nativity scene. I was also upset when people who didn't profess their Christianity during the year became almost fanatical Christians during the Christmas season.

I stopped identifying as a Muslim when I was about nineteen years old, which was difficult because the Lebanese culture didn't respect that. All I kept with me was a belief in the existence of God.

Once I was an adult and able to read English, I started reading more and more about Judaism and began to feel educated about the religion. Abraham is the one emotional element that links my early learning with my later studies of Judaism; Abraham, whose stories appear in the Koran, always fascinated me. During this time of study and reading, I began to relate to Judaism, especially because it is so pragmatic. Islam and Christianity don't offer the same opportunities to question everything as Judaism does. In fact, in Islam, questioning is simply not acceptable. In Judaism, however, you can question everything and you get answers.

It wasn't that I was lost and needed an identity; I feel that I am Jewish. When I started to build my mindset against the two religions that I knew about, I found myself much closer to Judaism; I related to Judaism.

Nour's Early Years

Nour: I was born in 1974 in Tripoli, Lebanon. When

I was growing up in Lebanon, we never saw any Jewish people. Although our family is Muslim, my father is very secular. I attended a non-religious school and while we didn't discuss religion, I had exposure to different Muslim and Christian holidays through my friends. There was a lot of intermarriage between Christians and Muslims in my mother's family. As a young girl, I wanted to study Islam in a special class with my good friend, but my father refused to allow those studies. He feared that I would be brainwashed or otherwise unduly influenced.

After I graduated from the University of Beirut, I pursued graduate studies in London. It wasn't until I was in graduate school that I knew anyone Jewish. I became very close friends with one Jewish woman who was a fellow student. When she wanted to visit me at home in Lebanon, I was excited to have her here. But my father, knowing how pervasive anti-Jewish attitudes are in Lebanon, said, "Look, we would love to have your best friend but do you really want to risk her life?" Her name was so Jewish that we feared the Lebanese government might consider her a spy from Israel or treat her badly in some other way. But meeting her allowed me to know more about Judaism and see someone Jewish for the first time. For the most part, Jews had left Lebanon before we were born; I think only about twenty or thirty Jews are registered now in Lebanon.

I am a mix of everything; I don't think of myself as 100 percent Muslim. I fast during *Ramadan* and I celebrate Eid, the feast marking the end of Ramadan, but we also celebrate with friends at Christmas. When I was younger, I accompanied my Christian friends to church and I celebrated with Muslim friends. Today, I am going to synagogue with Reda and I am a mixture of Christianity and Islam and Judaism. I am embracing what Reda is becoming and embracing that there is one God.

Transitioning to Judaism

Reda: About ten years ago, I began to reinvest more deeply into studying Judaism. Then, four or five years ago, I realized that it was literally impossible to convert if I stayed in Beirut. When we were still living in Lebanon but knew that we were moving to Washington, DC, I learned about Rabbi Weiss. I contacted her within days of moving here.

She could have thought I was a terrorist—I am Muslim-born and from Lebanon! In my e-mail, I delicately explained that I have been interested in Judaism for a long time and was interested in conversion. Within thirty minutes, Rabbi Weiss answered my e-mail; then we were talking on the phone.

I knew I had to choose one of three "flavors" of Judaism. Unquestionably, I can't be Orthodox, so that leaves Conservative or Reform Judaism. I knew that I wanted something in the middle and rooted in the essence of Torah; once I talked with Rabbi Weiss, I knew I wanted to experience the conversion process with her.

In my wildest dreams, I couldn't have imagined that Rabbi Weiss would be so straightforward with me; it felt too good to be true. Although I had some health problems, which made me very tired, studying with her was the highlight of my time. She has a unique style of being strong, outspoken, and present without being aggressive. She gets things done smoothly with her unique social "smarts" without anyone getting hurt. I am so lucky to have my rabbi possess values that I love—it's like I won the jackpot.

By converting to Judaism, I am embracing a culture, a community, everything. The conversion process with Rabbi Weiss is very personal and personalized; she tailors the lessons to the student's needs. She knows what comes first, what comes next, even without a curriculum to follow. She was unbelievably flexible with my health problems; I often texted her at the last minute to tell her that I couldn't show up for classes. She was never angry or disappointed; she always accommodated the time I lost because of my illness. My time with her is a kind of therapy; it's not just a lesson with a teacher, but a more human interaction.

At the end of the day, and I am talking about myself, I am converting because I want to convert. I know that people from my background will not like that I converted; some fanatic people will not like it. It doesn't matter. I am converting because of my belief. I consider myself a Jewish person, regardless.

My decision to convert to Judaism is very pragmatic and not at all romantic. I've been close to Judaism for a very long time; I feel that I am a Jew. In the United States, I am in a country where I can be part of a group or a synagogue that shares a certain belief with me. The God

I define and am comfortable with is unbelievably close to the Jewish God. It's a "no-brainer" for me to convert.

Progressive Views About Women

Reda: I believe in women's civil rights in marriage, which Islam doesn't recognize. Before Islam, women were considered "sub-zero," and with Islam, they are "zero."

Nour: Reda is atypical in many ways. We married under Islamic law, which usually permits only the man the right to divorce. He didn't want that, as he considered our relationship as being one of equals. He told the *Sheikh* (religious leader equivalant to a priest who is legally allowed to perform marriages) that he wanted both of us to marry with rights. In Islam, only men can get divorces, but Reda wanted both of us to have the right to split property and the right to divorce. The *Sheikh* had to consult with the *mufti* (a religious Sunni leader with more authority than a *Sheikh*) about Reda's demand. Although the *mufti* shot down the idea, we were married there nonetheless. Reda said that our being together is a joint decision; it's not just his decision or my decision. I would never be where I am in my career if he hadn't been so supportive and encouraging. He is very progressive about the treatment of women.

Reda: I have three older sisters and none of them have the kind of marriage that Nour and I have. I think that I would advocate for women's rights more than my sisters might.

I adore that Rabbi Weiss is a woman rabbi; I've never before had a strong woman who has achieved so much stand by my side. I've seen other strong and successful women, but I know how hard it must have been, even in the United States, for women of her generation to become rabbis. She is an outspoken yet kind and gentle rabbi.

The Jewish Community Embraces Them

Nour: Getting to know Rabbi Weiss and having her in our lives has been very positive. The first time we went to Rabbi Weiss's home for *Shabbat* (the Jewish Sabbath) dinner, I was very nervous. After all, we were born Muslim and we would be with Rabbi Weiss's students, most of whom had already converted. I wondered if they would accept us. How would they perceive us? Would it go well? I didn't have to worry, as it went well.

The Jewish community has been and remains so receptive and warm to us; Rabbi Weiss has embraced us so fully that we feel she is part of our family. Many of the rituals that Reda and I grew up with in Lebanon are rooted in Judaism, yet the politics of the region make it difficult, if not impossible, to acknowledge those similarities.

Lebanese Anti-Jewish Culture

Reda: In Lebanon, which went through the Six-Day War in June 1967 and the Yom Kippur War in 1973, there's no line drawn between Israelis and Jews. Many people there will say, "We hate Jews" when they really mean, "We hate Israelis," and vice versa.

In fact, in Lebanon, if Nour were to go to her family and tell them that I am converting to Judaism, she would automatically be divorced. She wouldn't need to ask for a divorce under Islamic law. From a Muslim perspective, the moment I convert to Judaism, we are divorced. Even converting from Islam to Christianity isn't easy for a Lebanese couple. Nour's supporting my decision to convert to Judaism is totally unheard of in our social circle.

If I were to return to Lebanon and someone found out that I was Jewish, I could be in trouble; I could be sent to prison. With the conflict between Lebanon and Israel and because Lebanese always associate Judaism with Israel, I could be considered a traitor or a spy.

Family Acceptance or Rejection?

Reda: The person I worry most about with my conversion is my father-in-law. I love him so much that I feel like he's my father, and he treats me like his son. But I can't share my decision to convert with him; that feels like a bigger burden than telling my brothers-in-law of my conversion. My conversion to Judaism would hit him the hardest because of Zionist issues. I can't characterize him as anti-Jewish, but he would believe in the conspiracy theories about Israel. My mother-in-law, however, would accept it. Because they live in Lebanon and we live in the United States, it makes it easier to live with this lie, yet harder to tell the truth—it's not a conversation we could ever have over the phone.

As a gay friend told me, this process is like coming out of the closet. I am sure my sisters will embrace it and accept it; they are the three individuals who are the most used to my different approach. Will they like it? Most will probably not, but they will accept it. I doubt that my brothers-in-law will accept my decision to convert, but I am leaving it to my sisters to decide whether they will share this decision with them or not. I will tell my sisters about my decision to convert before I meet with the *beit din* (rabbinical court of Jewish law) for my January 9, 2014, conversion ceremony.

In Lebanon, it is common practice to have two faces—a face at home and a public face; the public face has to respect the religion and culture, but I made a decision to be the same person privately and publicly; It took some time. My aunts and uncles judge me for that, and I minimize my contact with them. Sooner or later they will find out that I am Jewish, an illegal identity in Lebanon. That will not change my decision as I have waited for more than ten years to be Jewish. I can now publicly, proudly say that I am Jewish without giving it a second thought.

We have a *mezuzah* (prayer scroll in a small, decorative fixture affixed to the doorways of Jewish homes) on our door and most of our library is about Judaism—I am not hiding it. The vast majority of visitors to our apartment in Washington, DC, will positively admire my decision to convert.

Nour: There would be many ramifications to my father learning about Reda's decision. It's not just a secret that we're hiding, but it's how Judaism is perceived in the region and how it's associated with the conflict with Israel. My father grew up identifying as an Arab Socialist and has a belief that the Arab world is one united entity and that Palestine will one day be a part of that world. If we talked with my father for hours and hours, he might be able to accept Reda's conversion, as he is a very rational person.

Conflict Between Lebanon and Israel

Reda: I know many Israelis now; the Lebanese and the Israelis have so much in common—the same food and the same challenges with the constant fear of war; many Lebanese also believe that Hezbollah is hijacking the country.

Nour: The hatred is insane. We eat the same food and we both wonder, "Can't we have peace?" We can see Israel from Lebanon. At some point, you have to stop and look forward to the future.

Reda: We were once driving in Lebanon and saw signs for Palestine, when a guard stopped us and asked what we were doing there. We could see Kiryat Shmona and another settlement in Israel. We were so close that I could describe what kind of car someone was driving.

We need to live peacefully. When do we want to stop digging back into history? We have to recognize the past conflict and move on—like when two siblings have a problem and go their separate ways; when they reconcile, they never go back. They have to let past conflict go.

Nour: There would be so many opportunities if there were peace.

Reda: I can't see a single negative aspect to having peace between countries. We need to get over it and move on. I hate that Hezbollah uses people as human shields. I don't agree with all that Israel is doing or its decisions, but it's a legal state, a country.

I once argued with my sister about this and I asked her, "Have you ever spoken with a Palestinian living in the West Bank? Do you know what the civilians want?" Everyone I have ever met wants to get rid of Hamas; they would love to have Israel ruling all the country and allow them to keep their Palestinian identity. It's always people who are outside of a situation and not totally knowledgeable about an issue who comment. There are some shocking things happening, but they are happening on both sides of the conflict.

It amazes me how the word Zionism is considered worse than Satan in Lebanon. I don't agree with everything in Zionism, but like with any movement, I wouldn't agree with everything. That doesn't mean you deny the existence of the country. I am not totally 100 percent pro-Israel, but if it is doing something right, I should recognize it. It has an internal integrity; have you seen any Arab country trying its president for corruption as Israel did? Israel is progressive; while there are problems, it's a state that's working on itself.

I am not here to accuse or defend Israel. I agree with it and disagree with it on so many things, and it has nothing to do with Judaism. When I defend the Jews, people think I'm defending Israel.

Life in America after the Conversion Process is Complete

Reda: If I hadn't moved to Washington, DC, and given the chance to convert, I would have continued my connection to Judaism. I would love to have this identity of being a Jew. I am proud to say that I am Jewish. I only feel comfortable now interacting with people of my own beliefs. After I have converted, I will take more classes just to come back to Rabbi Weiss. I'm sure I will have several questions in the future.

Nour: I am very supportive of Reda. I enjoy the discussions we are having and reading a lot about Judaism, but I am not ready to convert. I enjoy the diversity of all religions.

Now that we're here in America, it's so easy. In Lebanon, things change drastically from one day to the next, so you can't go out without reading the news. Civilians are killed on the streets there. Here, I am cherishing being able to think about other things. My mind is free to wander.

Reda: Your entire perspective changes. If you want to survive in Lebanon, you must have a mindset that is always ready to change plans; the power may go out for several hours or Hezbollah will close down a city—these things keep you from planning your life. I am enjoying my peace of mind.

CHAPTER TWO

Daughter's Bat Mitzvah Inspires Mother to Act

Regrets Are Not What Make You Progress in Life

S oft-spoken and thoughtful, Vivienne speaks with a lyrical and lilting accent that hints of her native France. Married for twenty-five years to her Chilean-born husband, Roberto, Vivienne grew up in France, the daughter of a Caucasian, Catholic, and French mother and a mixed-race father. According to Vivienne, her parents are very secular; her mother disliked the disparity between the Catholic Church's teachings and the actual practices occurring in society, and her father grew up with a wide array of religious influences and had an interest only in the artistic aspects of religion.

After a brief visit to the United States during her senior year of high school, Vivienne returned a few years later, believing she would stay for only eighteen months or so. Thirty years later, she is still here; her time has included years of searching for a spiritual, political, communal home.

When they met, Vivienne and Roberto had both worked for the same large international development agency, perhaps a reflection of their foreign heritages. Feeling rootless during her youth, Vivienne noted that her parents carried the baggage of immigrants; perhaps she inherited or adopted that same sense of impermanence. She never felt like she had a home and she lacked exposure to religion during her childhood.

When she married Roberto, she knew little about Judaism and did not feel compelled to convert. Her husband was, as she described it, someone who practiced his Judaism at home rather than in a synagogue setting.

Vivienne Explains Her Family Background

Vivienne: I am a product of colonization in many ways. My maternal great-grandparents went to Algeria years before my mother was born there. They had been living in a rural area of France with barely enough food to eat. At that time, North African colonies were seeking settlers from France to come and work. As Algeria was a French colony, my mother was considered a French citizen born on foreign soil.

My father was from Martinique, which is part of France to this day. He came to France to study art. While there, he met my mother who had just left Algeria as the war of independence was about to break out. My parents, who were uprooted from a French territory where they were no longer needed or accepted, had an identity crisis. My father is of mixed race—Indian, French, black and white—and he was a product of the slave trade during which slaves were brought over to harvest sugar cane. My parents had to struggle with who they were; they were both very secular.

Although my mother was raised in a Catholic household, at a young age, she felt Catholicism was an incredibly contradictory, if not hypocritical, religion. She saw the church preaching values that weren't followed at home with her father's employees being exploited, Algerians' rights were exploited, and land taken from them.

My father was also secular, mostly because he came from a culture with many different influences, including voodoo. He was interested in the artistic aspects of religion, which he expressed through art and music.

When they had my brother and me, they planned no religion for us. My mother rejected Catholicism, the main religion of France, and my father was not interested in religious upbringing for his children. After my father left us—when I was six-months-old—my mother raised us alone. She felt very strongly about Judeo-Christian values and was strict in how she raised us. We didn't have to have a religion to respect the dignity and rights of others and to feel a connection with a higher being; she left us the option to search for our own religious aspirations, if we had any.

Strong Family Views on Atheism and Political Activism

Vivienne: Our atheist household held many values that were stricter than in some churchgoing households. My mother remarried, and my stepfather was very politically involved with trade unions as a prominent member of the Communist Party. We lived in the Parisian suburbs, and my mother and stepfather were teachers. We were considered rich, but we didn't aspire to wealth or physical comfort—the culture of the Communist Party was that the group was more important. Early on, we lived in a collective setting; my mother and stepfather worked long hours, and we went to summer camps and Easter camps. I went to my first camp when I was eighteen-months-old, and my brother and I worked as camp counselors at our first jobs.

My mother and stepfather demonstrated against the Vietnam War; it was hard for us to differentiate in France between the government and the people of America. Through the peace movement, we learned how strong the anti-war movement in the United States was. In 1968, when I was ten, my parents left us for about a month during the revolution in Paris. There's been much nos-

talgia ever since. We've never again experienced a time
when people have embraced such ideas.

Social Justice Issues Were an Entrée into Judaism

Vivienne: The transition to Judaism felt so natural to
me. Without knowing it, I had lived some of its values.
The political aspects of social justice, throughout my
young years, were hammered home. Judaism was a natural fit. I can't say that I had a plan for life. All my life, I
never had roots. I never knew who I was. I was not white,
I was not black, and I didn't fit in with my family or my
community. The only true connection was at the political
level. I had a long search for my identity, probably because France has many races. The area where I lived was
very tolerant of immigrants, and I felt like an immigrant
even though I was born there in France. My parents
came with the baggage of immigrants, and it took me a
long time to discover myself.

I worked in East Germany as an unskilled laborer
building hospitals with other young people from other countries. At one time, I considered moving to East
Germany, but it didn't happen. My mother insisted that
I attend my senior year of high school in a privileged
area of Paris, as she believed it would help me in college.
During that year, I visited the United States on a student
program and stayed with a strict Protestant family in
Boston for about ten days. I looked beyond the stereo-

types of the United States and what Americans should be. Even among well-to-do people, there appeared to be a wish to do social justice. I returned home and then came to the United States again when I was twenty-one or twenty-two. I came with my future husband, a German man, for eighteen months on a special visa and attended school in upstate New York where I mingled mostly with other foreign students.

A More Nuanced Understanding of America

Vivienne: Thirty years later, I am still here and I have changed my mind about the United States. I have a more nuanced understanding of American society and how tolerant it is; we didn't have that when I lived in France, with its very rigid society. Here, I was given space to evolve spiritually and psychologically; as a young adult, I had more opportunities here than if I'd stayed in France. I was an outsider here, but I was happier than I was in France. After 1968, French society became much more racist and intolerant. France and all of Europe always felt like a beacon for the rest of the world, but that's no longer the case. The United States has a healthier society than Europe does, but I don't think I'd ever considered converting to Judaism if I'd stayed in Europe. Catholicism is so strong in France. Here, I've discovered more diversity and, over time, I've had the chance to explore what would suit me.

The man I came to the United States with was my first husband. I met my second husband more than twenty-five years ago. We lived then in the Adams-Morgan neighborhood of Washington, DC, which we found appealing; its many Hispanic families and other foreigners reminded me of home. My husband, who is from Chile, and I realized we were seeking a place we could call home. I needed an anchor to grow a few roots; otherwise, it's very hard to function when you're always an outsider.

I knew immediately that he was Chilean but not that he was Jewish. Our first conversations were political, as my point of reference has always been political. I didn't know what his being Jewish meant. Over the years, however, I got to know his family and his culture, which was extremely Jewish, extremely secular, and suspicious of extremes. His mother was more religious. The men were more intellectually and traditionally, but not religiously, Jewish. My husband, Roberto, feels Jewish and lives his Judaism through work, travel, and everyday actions, but he doesn't pray because he doesn't feel the need to talk about God. I entered Judaism through the cultural and traditional aspects; I got to know the religious and spiritual aspects much later.

Judaism is a Religion for Everyday Life

Vivienne: Of course I am biased, but it seems to me that, except for Buddhism, Judaism is the only religion that can live in everyday life. There are no contradictions in not believing strongly in God or not even being sure about God but still being Jewish; I think that openness helped me find my way.

I've been with my husband for twenty-five years; our son just turned ninteen and our daughter is fifteen. They were raised with some Jewish traditions, but we didn't insist on religious schooling. When our daughter wanted to become a *bat mitzvah* (the coming-of-age ritual Jewish girls experience at twelve or thirteen years old), I had to do something to give her a choice. Two years ago, it felt quite natural for me to convert. Even though my in-laws didn't insist or bring it up, I felt like it was the right thing to do. I needed a deadline, as I had been thinking about it for five years or so. Our daughter's *bat mitzvah* gave me a time frame in which to accomplish it. I had heard, however, that it would be difficult to find a congregation that would accept me with all my questions, particularly since I wasn't sure about God's role.

After a very long search, my husband found Rabbi Weiss, and somehow it worked. I think Roberto knew a lot about Judaism, but he felt that people had an angle that was not his own. Being a Jew at home and doing his social justice work and being with various communities, but without one particular synagogue, was comfortable for him. In Chile, they all attended one synagogue and one school, which had a whole range of values. Here, each synagogue is more tailored to a particular view-point, and that has displeased him.

Rabbi Weiss Brings It All Together

Vivienne: Rabbi Weiss is so tolerant and incredibly good at listening and understanding people. In discussing other issues and through readings, she demonstrated a lot of Jewish values to me. Sometimes it takes a person like Rabbi Weiss to bring it all together; all those pieces were scattered and, in my case, there were decades of searching and thinking. The way she does her work is extremely compelling and helps you see the light in a way. When I was studying, I wasn't sure I was going to convert, but then things all became clear and made sense. I am still quite surprised about how this happened, though without Rabbi Weiss, it wouldn't have.

Even before we got married, I told Roberto I would be happy to convert and to join a synagogue, but his way was to do it at home and with no connection to a community. We had other ways of connecting with Jews, and some of our friends are really religious. Before my daughter had her *bat mitzvah,* she went to twenty-seven *b'nei mitzvah* (more than one bar mitzvah or more than one bar mitzvah and bat mitzvah) ceremonies. She then decided it was the right thing for her, so we found her a tutor.

Our daughter is now trying to figure out what to do. She's taking a break from going to synagogue after a very intense year. We joined a synagogue about eighteen months ago that has an unusual mix of Conservative and

Reform congregants. Our children are puzzled about
my decision to convert to Judaism, though I believe that
I must begin my spiritual journey alone. I attend synagogue services by myself. I'm the newest person in my
family to be Jewish, yet I'm the one who finds fulfillment
in a synagogue. It's taken me more than fifty years to
realize that spirituality and religion aren't just for those
who need a "crutch." I had fiercely resisted religious study
for many years, but the more I studied, the more I realized that Judaism is where I belong.

Leaving Regrets Behind

Vivienne: My only regret was that I should have converted twenty years ago, but regrets are not what make
you progress in life. I am still struggling with not forgiv-
ing myself for not having it done earlier, but I thought I
should have followed what my husband, who was almost
aloof about my converting, was saying. But if I had done
it back then, it would have changed a lot of things. When
you becomes a Jew, you can change your children's lives;
their identities are strengthened when both their parents
are Jewish. It gives them an anchor that I didn't have.
However, I am thinking that it's never too late—if I have
grandchildren, they will have a Jewish grandmother. My
children are older and it feels very strange for them that I
am now Jewish and sometimes they have trouble understanding that, but it's going to be fine.

I have a long way to go in becoming Jewish. I have to
work on that. I am in my spirituality's infancy stage, as I

barely know how to pray and I am searching for God. I am determined to be more open-minded and less certain that I know everything. If I allow myself to feel doubt, perhaps I will become more spiritual. My brother and I grew up believing that we were smarter than everyone else because we knew that God didn't exist; now, years later, I realize that maybe I was wrong.

I was extremely fortunate that my in-laws are so accepting; they never hinted that I should have converted earlier. When I did convert, I saw their joy and their happiness in my decision.

Going to Israel, where my husband has friends and family, was eye opening for me. I always had issues with the government, but I found enough people in Israel who were very respectful of the rights of Palestinians and who wanted to find a peaceful solution to a longstanding problem. For my husband, Israel is very much a part of his identity; it's his second country. I don't think he could live in Israel tomorrow, but if he had to, he could. I think I'd feel very comfortable living there because of the diversity of the people there. As for our children, we want them to spend time with youth groups in Israel so they can discover another aspect of Israeli culture and hopefully create friendships and bonds that will last a lifetime. At a *Shabbat* (the Jewish Sabbath) dinner, someone said that you don't have to love the government. You can respect the government, but you don't have to agree with it. Through your own actions, you can make progress. Ordinary citizens have a duty to see that, with voting, etc., evil things don't happen.

There are two aspects of Judaism for which I have very deep feelings. First, I feel honored to be part of that small group. I didn't think it would be an option to become Jewish; I am forever grateful. Many of my closest friends, who are also my husband's and in-laws' friends, are Jewish. Their shared attributes of commitment to family and Jewish culture always appealed to me. Second, this is quite pessimistic. In dark moments when I read about the re-emergence of anti-Semitism in Europe and I wondered what would happen if there was another Holocaust, I always felt that I would not want to be left behind. I don't like to consider a doomsday scenario, but if there was a knock on the door and my family was Jewish and I wasn't, I would not want the terrible privilege of being left behind. I feel that their struggle is my struggle; I came to Judaism through family and also community. That's where I belong, in the joyful part. If God forbid there were darker days for the Jews again, I would want to be there in the struggle and not as an outsider.

CHAPTER THREE

Moving from a Didactic Pentecostal Church to Welcoming and Questioning Judaism

Embracing His Sexuality, Eliyahu Returns to His Forefather's Religion

Eliyahu's journey to adulthood and embracing Judaism has been both extraordinarily challenging and remarkably affirming. Growing up in Charleston, South Carolina—where his family had lived for centuries—as a closeted gay boy, he was immersed in his family's Pentecostal Christian religious practices. Ironically, his father's family was Jewish when they first arrived in Charlestown, but the first generation of sons born in the United States married Christian girls and converted. Since then, the family has remained Christian.

Ebullient and enthusiastic, Eliyahu has embraced Judaism with as much passion and commitment as he has devoted to his career in musical theater. A leader in the Kabbalah movement in the Washington, DC, area, Eliyahu served as a rabbi (rabbi means teacher) of Jewish holidays and observances for his fellow cast members even before his conversion to Judaism.

Although his family was highly critical of his same-sex marriage and his conversion to Judaism, Eliyahu has invested a great deal of emotional energy toward reconciling with his parents. He and his partner are creating a Jewish home for themselves and, perhaps, for the grandchildren his partner's father so desires.

Eliyahu Speaks

Eliyahu: When I was growing up, I was always told, "Seek God and you'll find God." I sought and Judaism is what I found. Before my parents married, my father was a loosely religious Baptist. My mother, however, wouldn't go on a date with him without a chaperone. She grew up in a very strict Pentecostal sect; women weren't permitted to cut their hair or wear makeup or jewelry, and their skirts had to come to their ankles. Pentecostal Church of God, which is what our family followed, was slightly more relaxed. At our church, dancing, singing, and talking in tongues were the norm. It also had very strict expectations: "Dos" get you into heaven; "don'ts" get you into hell. We were not allowed to question anything.

I was not a well-behaved child at church, but one event captured my attention when I was about nine years old. During Easter, a rabbi and his son, who was about my age, came to our children's church service to explain Passover and the *Seder* (the Passover ritual meal to observe the liberation of the Jews after being exiled from Egypt and wandering in the desert for forty years. Seder means "order" as there is a precise order of the readings that are recited before and after the holiday meal). I was engrossed with what they were saying; something about their words just resonated with me.

In middle school and high school, I was very involved with our church's projects to help people overseas and in the United States. I was engaged in *tikkun olam* (healing or repairing the world through good acts or good deeds). I just didn't know then that it was an integral aspect of living a Jewish life. In Venezuela, we helped build a medical clinic and housing. In North Dakota, we helped rehab a church on a Native American reservation. We led vacation Bible services and revival services at a struggling church in New York.

At Lee University, a Pentecostal Church of God college in Cleveland, Tennessee, I realized that I couldn't keep my sexuality secret any longer. People who attended the college were passionately connected with the Church of God and its belief system, yet I was secretly dating a man at the college. I'd known forever—probably since I was six or seven—that I was different; other boys were getting curious about girls, and I wasn't.

Forced Out of the Closet

Eliyahu: The gay rights movement was vehemently condemned at Lee, which had a strict demerit system. A woman would receive ninety-five demerits for getting pregnant; dancing earned the offenders ninety-six demerits. Anyone who was found to be gay automatically received one hundred demerits and was thrown out of school and shunned. As a music major and theater minor, I was part of several traveling drama ministry teams and choirs. When I felt like I was going crazy about keeping my sexuality a secret, I talked with one professor who referred me to campus services. That professor promptly turned me into the dean. Although I was allowed to finish the semester, I was kicked out of the drama ministry and stripped of my scholarship. The school called my parents to tell them that I was gay.

I didn't want to be gay. I was taught that it was wrong. Instead of helping me with my struggle, everyone at Lee wanted to get rid of me and pushed me away. Once I was home, my parents couldn't look me in the eye, and I wasn't permitted to perform musically at our home church.

When we walked into church, we could feel the wake of gossip behind me. It was devastating. I thought these people were part of my extended family, yet they turned on me so suddenly. I had believed that when someone is hurting and looking for help, you reach out to that person to help, yet that's the opposite of what I experienced. During this tumultuous time, I felt very desperate and confused. I didn't know if I was supposed to try to change my sexuality or to learn to love myself. People in the church were condemning me; I was connected with God but not with the church. So it was no surprise that I started backing away from the tradition in which I'd grown up. My aunt was involved with an Episcopal church, and I began to sing with its choir. The church's structure and formality comforted me, as everything else was in chaos at the time. Eventually, when I grew to a point of needing more than the church could offer me, I began searching for a spiritual home.

New York City's Kabbalah Centre is Welcoming

Eliyahu: I transferred to New York University to complete my education as a theater major while working fulltime at a Starbucks. Still on a spiritual search, I looked at lots of books on religious traditions at every Barnes & Noble or second-hand bookstore I passed. Nothing connected for me until a co-worker suggested I look into Kabbalah, explaining that a cousin of hers had been positively transformed by her involvement with Kabbalah. Intrigued, I picked up some books about Kabbalah and something drew me in—the Hebrew and

Aramaic and the Zohar and Torah really drew me in. At a Kabbalah Centre open house in Manhattan, I was hugged and welcomed; no one ever looked askance at me for being gay. Almost immediately, I felt like I had a home where people expressed so much unconditional love. The Kabbalah Centre has taught me that miracles are present in our daily lives; it's up to us to recognize and appreciate them.

After I took classes there for about six months, I was much happier and more grounded; my boy-friend—now my husband—wanted the same thing for himself, so he came and studied Kabbalah with me. It's a very spiritual form of Judaism; we don't do things for tradition's sake. Our prayers, songs, and rituals are inculcated with spirituality. A focus solely on tradition discounts the power of our connection to God. Kabbalah places a huge emphasis on volunteering and helping other people; we're all one community under Kabbalah. I think that touched me the most, as I needed that the most when I was hurting. With studying texts and learning, it can be easy to get wrapped up only in the cerebral world of study and spiritual exploration; it can be easy to forget that we have to turn this learning into action. If it's not changing us or driving us to something positive or to help someone, the study is pointless. At the Kabbalah Centre, which emphasizes spiritual, not religious, connections, I was surrounded by Jewish people and loving it. I'd attend *Kabbalat Shabbat* (reception of the Shabbat) services on Friday nights and Torah services on Saturday mornings. Even though I couldn't understand the prayers, I'd just listen, look, and absorb the energy of it all. It was like a *mikveh* (bath used for the purpose of ritual immersion) of spirituality with people.

At one Torah service, I turned to Michael and said, "I want to be Jewish. I know I don't need to convert, but I want to be a Jewish person and take on the responsibility of connecting." My teacher at the Kabbalah Centre, which doesn't perform conversion ceremonies, told me to study the different denominations of Judaism, find a rabbi, and understand that it is a long process. "Be persistent," he told me, as some rabbis will reject you before they say "yes" to your desire to convert.

It was ironic: At the same time I had committed to becoming a Jew, I was in the touring company of *Jesus Christ Superstar,* and I had to sing about Jesus Christ, including one show held on Yom Kippur! Along with my Kabbalistic studies, I began learning on my own more about Judaism and history so that I'd be prepared when the conversion process began. Before I even met Rabbi Weiss, I had probably read more than three-fourths of the books on her list for her conversion students. Long before I converted, I realized that I should be able to give up pork and shellfish and keep meat and milk meals separate. It can be difficult to do that on tour—when the bus stops at fast food places—but I did the best I could. I also started wearing a *kippah* (head covering that many Jewish men and some Jewish women wear) on a regular basis. During one year, the entire company came together for a Passover *Seder* that I led.

Finding a Spiritual Home in Judaism

Eliyahu: Initially, I thought that I wanted an Orthodox conversion, but I had a very negative experience with one Orthodox rabbi; he insisted on a ten thousand dollar fee and demanded I commit to a life of celibacy before he would engage with me. When I explained that I couldn't afford that fee, he challenged my commitment to and motivation for conversion. I took a brief respite and did some soul-searching to evaluate the rabbi's assertion. I realized my motivations were right, but I simply wasn't wealthy. I knew that when I found the right person to help me convert, it would happen.

After several years of living in New York City, Michael and I relocated to Washington, DC, where he found a job. It was a completely new city for me that didn't seem very Jewish, at least on the surface, so I started exploring. I've found my spiritual and religious connection with the large Kabbalah study group here in DC, which is my spiritual home here. I also occasionally attended *Shabbat* (the Jewish Sabbath) services at the Sixth and I Historic Synagogue. That's where I learned about Rabbi Weiss's course, Basic Judaism for Jews and Non-Jews Alike. From the very first class, I felt a connection to her. When I asked her if I could study with her one-on-one for my conversion, she said, "Come."

None of my family attended our wedding, and some family members said some hurtful things after our

marriage. Rabbi Weiss helped me reach out and reconnect with my family and show them who I am. It's been
a slow road, but I've experienced some beautiful, healing
moments with some of them. Michael's father, who was
unsupportive of Michael's sexuality for many years, now
can't wait for us to have a child.

On the morning of my conversion in 2011, I remember being nervous about whether I merited a "yes" from
the *beit din* (rabbinical court of Jewish laws). One of the
rabbis noted that he couldn't recall another conversion of
someone living such a strong Jewish life pre-conversion
as I was doing. Some of my Jewish friends asked why I
would convert; I thought, "Why wouldn't I?" Many of
them weren't taught the beautiful spiritual concepts of
Judaism as I have learned.

The practice within Judaism that most attracted me is
"Why?" It's required of us to ask those questions; if we're
not, we're doing something wrong. In the Pentecostal
Church, where everything in the Bible is taken literally,
questioning is not permitted. In Judaism, an ancient rabbi wrote that every line in the Torah can be interpreted in
seventy different ways . . . and all seventy are correct.

As the study group leader for the Kabbalah group in
DC, I'm the lay rabbi of that community. I'm neither a
rabbi nor an official teacher, but I'm able to help students
connect with teachers from the Kabbalah Centre in New
York and to answer their questions. I love their questions. To be able to help students on their journey is very
rewarding.

Coming to Judaism was such a long slow study process and a gradual accepting of *mitzvot* (plural of *mitzvah*, which means "commandment or obligation under Jewish law) even before I became Jewish. It was challenging for me to figure out what the Messiah meant to me, as I'd grown up in such a Jesus-centric environment. I am easily identified as a Jew, as I wear my *kippah* all the time. As such, I did experience some anti-Semitism here from some street preachers, even before my conversion. I felt very much a Jew then, and I realized anti-Semitism is part of it. Who knows what kind of government we might have thirty years from now. I think about World War II and the *Shoah* (the Holocaust) often. Even as a child, I thought that maybe in a previous life, I had been there in war-torn Europe. It wasn't just a story or a history class for me. If it came to that, I would hold onto my faith and fight to be a Jew.

Israel is the Beginning of the World

Eliyahu: Israel is the spiritual energy center of the world. Even though we don't have the presence of the Temple there anymore, its physical energy is there. I don't know what to expect in Israel. I want to learn everything there is and talk to people and hear lectures and study texts there and to visit some graves and light a candle and connect with that ancient history.

In Israel, the air is different, the land is different, and the water is different. I know that, even without having visited. I very much want to visit Israel when I can afford to make the trip. Why else would there be so much political strife and so many wars over this tiny piece of land if it weren't unique compared to other countries in the entire world? Smaller than New Jersey, Israel offers everything you can experience around the world—from deserts to mountain skiing, vineyards and ocean views, and the Dead Sea. It's the beginning of the world.

For me, the Kabbalah Centre is home, as are Israel and Rabbi Weiss. During her rabbinical studies in Israel, she was supposed to be on a bus that was blown up by a suicide bomber. Fortunately, she had taken a different bus that day. When she wondered aloud why she hadn't been on that bus, I reminded her that she'd helped so many people experience conversion. Rabbi Weiss had told me that when you open someone's eyes by helping them convert or make a change for the better, you create a new world every time it happens. She created all those new worlds, which wouldn't have come into existence if she'd been on the bombed bus.

I had strongly connected to the name Elijah/Eliyahu, but I wasn't sure if the name was right for me. After several weeks of meditation about it, the senior rabbi at the Kabbalah Centre confirmed that Eliyahu, a name of leadership, was the right name for me. "After all," he said, "the name is quite appropriate for you, as you are our leader in Washington, DC." My name was reaffirmed.

CHAPTER FOUR

A Forty-Year Journey to Find Judaism

Accomplished Professional's Career Inculcated with Jewish Values

A force to be reckoned with, Miriam has embraced the new life she has found in Judaism. After becoming disillusioned with Catholicism, the religion in which she was raised, she began studying with me. Shortly after she converted to Judaism, she wholeheartedly immersed herself in the life of a Reform synagogue: Attending Friday night and Saturday morning *Shabbat* (the Jewish Sabbath) services, participating in a weekly Torah study group, becoming a *bat mitzvah* (the coming-of-age ritual Jewish girls expereince at twelve or thirteen years old)

chairing the synagogue's social action committee, and serving on the membership committee and on the national organization Women of Reform Judaism!

Miriam's leadership in her synagogue is not surprising; she has held increasingly responsible positions in nursing with the US Department of Defense, and at many times throughout her career, she effectuated policy changes that bettered healthcare for those serving in the military. Miriam's many contributions to *tikkun olam* (healing or repairing the world through good acts or good deeds) predated her conversion to Judaism. Forever blessed to have had her as a student, I find it heartwarming to see Miriam's robust participation in and commitment to an observant and engaged Jewish life, both within and outside of her synagogue. I am delighted to see her ebullience, energy, and infectious enthusiasm for "all things Jewish."

Miriam Shares Her Story

Miriam: Like Moses in the desert, I found Judaism—after forty years of Catholic schooling and searching. Converting to Judaism and finding Rabbi Weiss totally changed my life. My sister says that she's never seen me happier.

Both my mother and father were in the Army; they met when my father was recovering in a military hospital in Alabama after he'd been seriously wounded. Born in 1947, I was the first of four girls, and my father, who is of Irish descent, named me Patricia after St. Patrick,

Ireland's patron saint.

My mother's family was very Catholic and of Scottish, Irish, and English heritage, but their roots in America date back to the Mayflower. My father's parents were Catholics and very observant of all the rituals. When I was growing up, our dinner table guests included local priests. Easter dinner meant ham while Christmas dinner meant turkey, and we followed the Catholic Church's edict of "no meat on Friday." Our Christmas morning schedule began with Mass, then breakfast. Only then could we open the presents under the Christmas tree.

Back in the '40s and '50s, we had a real awareness of ethnicity—someone was Italian, someone else was Polish, and someone else, Irish. I knew very few African-Americans and I never knew how Jews observed holidays. Most families were intact. I didn't know families affected by divorce. I grew up in a cocoon, in an old-fashioned lifestyle. We recited the Lord's Prayer and saluted the flag.

I went through all the sacraments in the Catholic Church. When I was very young, we moved from New York City to northern New Jersey. The few Jewish kids I knew were always the real smart kids. Our Jewish Girl Scout troop leader taught us how to make *hamantashen* (a triangular cookie made during Purim, a festive Jewish holiday); I didn't know then what they were called, but I knew them, however, as delicious triangular cookies! When I was ten, my father died and we moved to Cape Cod, Massachusetts. Then, it was something of a desolate wasteland; it was pretty but sparsely populated. I don't think there were any Jews living there then.

Rejecting Catholicism

Miriam: The nuns who taught at my Catholic high school were wonderful, but I was really turned off by the Catholicism I witnessed in the Catholic college I attended. We were told that women were the princesses of the Church, yet we could only study nursing or education and were told that we, as women, were the roots of all evil. We weren't permitted to wear slacks, even on the coldest winter days; it was just ridiculous. There were so many negative things.

The turning point, I think, came at a mass during my freshman year. Every Sunday we heard a financial report but nothing uplifting. The church wanted to build a new altar out of Carrera marble and for us women to donate our jewelry so they could melt it down to create a new chalice. It was ridiculous and I started laughing. It hit me all wrong—the priests were all driving Lincoln Continentals and they wanted our jewelry! Hearing those messages of "Do as I say, not do as I do" was very transformative for me; I really found the entire experience unappealing. Eventually, I wandered into never-never land and didn't practice any religion.

I had some exposure to Jewish issues during nursing school in Boston. Not only did I work at a Jewish delicatessen where I developed a good sense for Jewish culture and food, but I also got to know some Jewish medical students and doctors, mostly from Tufts University School of Medicine. They were attentive and caring; medicine didn't seem to be about money for them. They seemed to care more about treating and healing their patients, which impressed me. They were a big early influence on my interest in Judaism.

I read *Jews, God, and History* by Max Dimont when I was twenty-four, and I had some Jewish friends, including some Jewish boyfriends. But I think the Jewish doctors were the biggest influence on me. There was something down-to-earth about the Jews I knew; I liked their lack of pretentiousness and their intelligence.

I'd been seeking something more spiritually appealing and welcoming than what I found in the Catholic Church. My daughter's Catholic school was extremely unhelpful and unsupportive after she was diagnosed with diabetes. Then, the church that was associated with the second Catholic school she attended told me that we weren't allowed to join, simply because we lived in the wrong zip code. I was just appalled and couldn't believe that geography would dictate where we could worship; you can't make this stuff up! That experience was a big turnoff, and I had no tolerance for the child molestation scandals.

I'd had Jewish boyfriends who were secular and always appreciated Jewish humor. I was definitely searching for something spiritual, as Catholicism wasn't working for me. I was married briefly to a man wholly invested in Christian proselytizing—so much so that he was fired from his job because of it. He became very irrational and focused all his attention on trying to get people to become Christian.

When I first walked into a synagogue in 2009, my

life was forever changed. I had noticed the Star of David in the window of a synagogue known as Sixth and I in Washington, DC, which at one point had been an AME church. I had asked some friends if I could join them there. That first visit to the synagogue just blew me away. Members of an African-American church also attended the service to remember the late Dr. Martin Luther King, Jr. The multi-generational congregants at Sixth and I were so warm, so welcoming that I felt up-lifted and embraced. I was intrigued by that first experience at the synagogue.

Embracing a Synagogue

Miriam: Not long after that, I was on the Metro and saw an ad in a free newspaper for an introductory Judaism class at The Washington Institute for Conversion and the Study of Judaism. I took the class, which is how I found Rabbi Weiss. Then, I began studying privately with her in 2009. I had my conversion on June 11, 2010, and I became a *bat mitzvah* on May 19, 2012. After studying with Rabbi Weiss, I went looking for a synagogue. I tried two other synagogues, but when I visited one Reform synagogue in suburban Virginia, I said, "This is it. This is home. Look no further." At my first visit, the synagogue had a display of the history of Judaism in Washington, DC; as a history buff, I was totally enamored with the exhibit. The congregants were so warm and welcoming that I felt embraced, and the cantor sang like an angel!

Some congregants suggested I try Torah study sessions, which I did. Then, someone recommended I attend Saturday morning services, which I did. I still take Hebrew classes—I need to work harder to learn the language, I think—and participate in Torah class. I was nominated to be on the board, which surprised me, as I'm not sure I was ready; however, I am now the secretary of the board. I also participated in a leadership class, and I chair the social action committee. I am involved, as well, in Women of Reform Judaism, a national organization committed to social justice issues.

Being Jewish is the "happy dance" for me; it's been transformative for me. Sometimes I get jealous of people who grew up with Judaism or who converted at a younger age than I did. Jewish entities offer so many social outlets. I think that Judaism is a more wholesome religion that embraces and welcomes people of all generations. If I'd converted when I was younger, I would have had good Jewish children. It's a very positive way to live. It's ironic that after my husband and I divorced, my daughter and I would celebrate Christmas with a movie and then dinner at a Chinese restaurant, which is a classic way that Jews celebrate Christmas!

Rabbi Weiss is so generous with her time and her wisdom that she creates a nurturing atmosphere, one that also offers her students a strong intellectual and spiritual foundation. But if it wasn't for her, I don't know that I would have continued with my studies; she asked me questions that no one had ever asked me before. Rabbi Weiss is the glue that holds all her students together—we feel this amazing bond and connectedness of Jewishness, thanks to her. She's such a pioneer, and while I've had some pioneering experiences of my own, I haven't done anything like what she's done. I learn so much at her *Shabbat* dinners; she's got such a big heart and a lot of brain, too! Even after converting, I've not been cut off; Rabbi Weiss maintains warm and caring relationships with her students.

I probably could have fit in at most synagogues, but the people at my synagogue drew me there; I feel surrounded by all the generations. I recognize the differences among the Judaism movements, but I don't feel tension around them. I've gone to Reconstructionist and Orthodox synagogues, but at my Reform synagogue, I am comfortable in my own skin. The synagogue is my home; it's my spiritual and social home. I really enjoy the Jewish cultural events—the film festivals, concert series, etc.—at the Jewish Community Center.

I don't keep kosher, but I am mindful of the "no meat and milk" kind of things. Although I love lobster and other shellfish, I don't eat them anymore. I'm choosing what to eat and what not to eat, but I don't make it onerous for myself.

Sharing the Decision to Convert

Miriam: I shared the news at work with my Jewish colleagues and a secretary. As for my immediate family, only one of my sisters knows I converted; she came for my *bat mitzvah*. One sister is an evangelical Christian and another sister's husband is an evangelical minister. I

don't want to cut off these relationships. I think it would
be a struggle for them to understand my decision.

My mother, who is still a devout Catholic at eighty-
nine, asked which church I usually attend. I said that I
don't go. She does know, however, that my boyfriend is
Jewish. My mother, who recently stayed with me for two
months, didn't comment on the *mezuzah* (prayer scroll
in a small, decorative fixture affixed to the doorways of
Jewish homes) on my front door (which I had before I
became Jewish), the *menorahs* (candlestick holder used
in Jewish worship that holds seven candles), my whole
section of Jewish books, or my *Passover* dishes. She hasn't
asked any questions yet; it may be that she's in denial or
it may be that she simply doesn't see my items of *Judaica*
(jewlery, art, textiles, etc. from Israel). She calls Catholicism the only true religion, but I just don't go there with
her; it's not worth it. It's a strain for me because I haven't
told her. I guess we've never had a close relationship. At
home, I was the good girl who cleaned house and earned
good grades; later, I went to boarding school. After my
father died, she remarried when I was in high school, but
it was a horror show because she never had time to listen
to me. I feel closer to Rabbi Weiss than I do to my mother. I don't explain my choice to be a Jew with my mother.
I trust in God, I pray to God, and I don't believe we'll be
punished for not believing in a particular religion. I don't
know what happens after we die. Judaism is about living
a good life now, not about delayed gratification.

My twenty-seven-year-old daughter supports my
decision. I'm not sure if she practices any religion. Life

is short. I'm someone who thinks, "Why can't we all get along?" I think my daughter and sister think that, too. Sometimes I think the industrious and hardworking Jews make other people look bad; I know it's a stereotype, but . . . I've tried to be sensitive to other people's feelings about religion, but I also want to live my life.

Practicing Jewish Values Even Before a Conversion

Miriam: I think I was struck early on by the Jewish concepts of loving-kindness and caring for those who need help; I feel like I try to practice those all the time. My heart goes out to people who, through no fault of their own, need help. That's why the social action committee appeals to me. We've been collecting food and helping with a domestic violence shelter. Last year, I participated in a program called Good Deeds Day, which is an annual, international day of service that an Israeli woman began several years ago. I took on the responsibility of making pillowcases for children with cancer. This year, I'm going to do a *mitzvah* (commandment or obligation under Jewish law) a day and make 365 pillowcases using kid-friendly fabric. Some forty thousand children in the United States are hospitalized annually with cancer. I love Maimonides's idea that giving anonymously to an unknown recipient is one of the best and most meaningful acts of loving-kindness. That's what we're doing with my pillowcases and with our social action work.

We were poor after my father died, and I don't remember any handouts or help. We'd only have macaroni and cheese at the end of the month. I remember my legs just "killing me" after those long days of working my way through high school and college as a waitress. And as a nurse, I've seen traumatized or disabled patients; they could be any of us. It's important to help.

Jews were really the most focused on having a code of laws and following the obligations of *tzedakah* (to perform acts of charity or donate money). We simply should not deny care to those in need. That's why I think Obama's Affordable Care Act is so valuable. When I worked in Boston, I saw heartbreaking cases of ill individuals with diagnoses that might have been curable with earlier treatment. When I worked at an inner-city hospital, I noticed that it often had inadequate resources to effectively treat its poverty-stricken patients.

Being a leader in the synagogue is a chance to make things happen to better someone's life and, as a commanding officer in the Navy, I've had some practice being a leader. I donated money to build a cabinet to hold supplies for our social action committee so now there's a Miriam Social Action Cabinet. Because I want more youth engagement at the synagogue, I hope to develop a certificate program to recognize kids who put some real energy and effort into their *bar* or *bat mitzvah* service project. One student's presentation for his project—raising money for African communities to drill wells for fresh water—was so impressive that it was like something you'd see in an MBA program. The kids studying for their respective *bar* or *bat mitzvah* are so well-prepared, and they focus on social action. Watching them lead the service and hearing their essays is uplifting. Even so, I'd like to see students who do extraordinary work be recognized.

Healing Patients

Miriam: I've had such a depth and breadth of nursing experiences in my career; now, I'm working in a more administrative role. During the course of my career, I established a program for women that evaluated perinatal outcomes and created an education program for women during pregnancy and each baby's first year of life. I was a military nurse when the military began AIDS testing in the mid-1980s. Then, if someone tested HIV-positive, he or she was told the news by the commanding officer. I changed that. There was no way a line officer should know such private information. I wrote the regulation to change it; now a doctor relays that information. I remember one congressman asking me how many military men in his district were HIV-positive. I refused to tell him.

Years ago, military victims of rape were billed for the cost of the rape kits. Although Army officials believed that this was wrong and shouldn't be done, we couldn't change the policy without changing the law. I wrote it all up; it took four years, but we did it—we changed the law. Now, a program reimburses the hospital for the cost of the rape kits. I just wanted to make sure that patients didn't get billed. I couldn't imagine how horrible it would have been to be billed for that.

I chose Miriam as my Hebrew name because Miriam was like a nurse to her brother Moses and she nurtured him. I liked that connection, even though she wasn't one of the matriarchs. It fit me. I appreciate the honesty of the people in the Bible. They were humans, not saints.

Views of the Holocaust Views of Israel

Miriam: I have never gotten over the Holocaust. When we lived in New Jersey, my mother told me that a family who lived across the street from us wouldn't be alive now if they had been in Germany. I was ten then, and I remember thinking, "That's so wrong."

When I was thirteen, I tried to read *The Rise and Fall of the Third Reich*, but my mother took it away from me. I read *The Diary of Anne Frank* and several other books with very graphic descriptions of how Jews were treated. There was never any reason for this to happen, but the churches allowed it to continue. How could they treat human beings that way? They've given so much more to the world—in law, science, and education. There's no reason that they should have been treated that way.

Even today, I am deeply affected and moved when someone tells me he or she is a Holocaust survivor; I always remember my mother's explanation about our neighbors' situation. Since I've worked with Vietnam veterans who had Post-Traumatic Stress Disorder (PTSD), I understand some of the stress that affects survivors and children of survivors. Some of Germany's common people were willing executioners; Hitler wasn't the only one. I haven't encountered any anti-Semitism yet—perhaps because I "don't look Jewish"—but some of the people I love are anti-Semitic.

Even before converting, I was a pro-Israel Zionist, and I am even more so now, after the reading I've done. When you think of everything the Jews did to make the desert fertile and productive . . . all that hard work. The Saudis and other Arabs have never negotiated anything; it seems to me that it's always "no" or "no action" with them. We've been homeless, we've tried to assimilate into other homelands, and we have been persecuted for it. We need a homeland!

Rabbi Weiss epitomizes loving kindness; I want to live up to Judaism's highest ethics because of her. She is such a shining light and has totally transformed my life. The entire experience—of studying and converting—has been such a privilege.

CHAPTER FIVE

Professional Colleagues Meet, Fall in Love, and Wed

Can a New Jersey Jew and a Midwestern Catholic Find Happiness?

When **Aaron and Ahava participated** in my course Basic Judaism for Jews and Non-Jews Alike, I quickly realized that each expressed a sweet affection and support for the other. Aaron and Ahava, both of whom are bright, intellectually curious, and attractive, seemed to be a perfectly matched couple even before they became engaged. I was delighted that Aaron, raised as a Reform Jew from New Jersey, came to class to support Ahava, who ultimately decided to convert to Judaism before she and Aaron were married. Like many of my other students, Ahava came to embrace Judaism because she'd fallen in love with Aaron, who also attended and participated in Ahava's conversion study sessions. Aaron explained that he found the process of studying Judaism as an adult enlightening and worthwhile.

Ahava, who grew up as a nominally observant Catholic, found embracing Aaron's religion a straightforward and positive process, perhaps because her family and Aaron's family enthusiastically supported her decision. In fact, members of both families came to Ahava's *mikveh* (bath used for the purpose of ritual immersion).

The young newlywed couple believes that having a Christmas tree in their home does not conflict with being Jewish. As Ahava explained, "We always celebrate Christmas with my family and I don't think there's anything harmful in continuing traditions. There's a good chance that we will have a Christmas tree in our home. Traditions were part of what drew me to Judaism . . . we go to High Holidays services in New Jersey with Aaron's family."

Aaron Explains How They Met

Aaron: We started work at a political consulting firm in Washington, DC, on the same day in July 2007. We began dating about a year later, although we kept it a secret at work for quite a while. We got engaged in 2011 and were married in December 2012.

Ahava and Her Family Were "Creaster" Catholics

Ahava: The Bible is pretty sassy, but you don't realize that until you're older. I have one older and one younger sister; we grew up in the suburbs of Chicago, Illinois. My mother ran a catering business out of our home so she could be home with us. My father was a mailman. Although my father was a Eucharistic minister who attended church nearly every Sunday, the rest of us were "Creaster" Catholics who never missed a Christmas or Easter service. We focused more on Catholicism's traditions, including those of music and food, and less on the religious aspects. I attended Catholic parochial school throughout fourth grade.

Although one of my best friends was Jewish, she wasn't observant, so I didn't learn anything about Judaism then. In fact, I had more exposure to Islam because my mother's catering company cooked for the Islamic Cultural Center.

In high school and in college, I took theology classes. In college, I enrolled in many art classes, which incorporate religion, and religion classes. As a big reader, I'd always been fascinated by the history and politics of different religions. When I studied abroad, I learned about Jewish history and visited a Nazi labor camp in Belgium.

Aaron Inculcated in Jewish Traditions

Aaron: I grew up in a heavily Jewish town in northern New Jersey that had three synagogues—one Reform, one Conservative, and one Orthodox. I am still close to the rabbi at our Reform synagogue, so much so that I didn't feel the need to be involved in *Chabad* (a Jewish outreach organization unaffiliated with the Reform, Conservative, or Orthodox movements) or *Hillel* (a college-based Jewish program) at Syracuse University.

Although I knew plenty of non-Jewish kids, most of my close friends when I was growing up were Jewish. In fact, during my *bar mitzvah* (the coming-of-age ritual Jewish boys experience at thirteen years old) year, I think I attended a *bar* or *bat mitzvah* (the coming-of-age ritual Jewish girls experience at twelve or thirteen years old) every weekend with the exception of one or two; at my synagogue alone, thirty kids became *bar* or *bat mitzvah* that year. When I was growing up, I participated in virtually every sports team available. Most of the kids who attended the summer camp I went to were Jewish, but it wasn't a traditional Jewish camp; it focused more on sports. After my *bar mitzvah*, I participated in confirmation class where we talked about Jewish cultural and social justice issues—including the death penalty—to challenge our perspectives and develop our values.

As a family, we regularly celebrated the High Holy Days of Rosh Hashanah and Yom Kippur as well as *Suk-*

kot and Passover with extended family. My experiences of attending services with my family, conversations with our synagogue's rabbi, and visiting relatives during holidays filled my religious needs in college where I focused more on classes, sports, and leadership positions.

Love Leads Ahava to Exploring Judaism

Ahava: Like many people, I probably never would have considered studying and converting to Judaism if I hadn't fallen in love with a Jewish man. Since I wasn't particularly religious, Aaron's religion was a non-issue for me. The closer we grew, the more I wanted to learn about Judaism; I know how important his religion is to him. I started my education by talking with friends who are in interfaith relationships and by reading about traditions and holidays. Gaining this knowledge, of course, made attending holiday meals and services more comfortable for me, as I knew and understood the traditions and rituals a bit better.

After we were together for a few years, we began discussing marriage and children. Although I knew that Aaron had envisioned marrying someone Jewish, I also knew that he loved me and that we were going to spend our lives together, no matter my religion. Aaron never once asked or encouraged me to convert; the decision was wholly mine. Aaron's decision to defer the choice to me and my knowing that we would marry made my decision to convert easier. We also agreed that we'd raise our children in the Jewish religion. After talking with a friend's mother—a Protestant who converted to Catholicism, which was the religion of her husband and children—I decided I wanted to enroll in an introductory Judaism class.

Soon after that, Aaron and I met with his family rabbi during a visit to his family in New Jersey. Fearful of raising unrealistic expectations for Aaron or his family or of letting them down in some way, I was greatly relieved when we talked with him. Not only did he never push me, he gave me information and told me the Jewish people would be honored to count me among their ranks. He also offered to marry us even if I chose not to convert, although I knew that I wanted to be the same religion as our children. Aaron's rabbi suggested I enroll in an introductory class in Judaism. I read the materials he gave me and thought about his recommendation; several months later, I stumbled upon Rabbi Weiss's classes.

When I told Aaron I planned to enroll in Rabbi Weiss's class Basic Judaism for Jews and Non-Jews Alike, he told me he wanted to take the class with me. I was both touched and relieved that he chose to do so; it meant the world to me. I've also received so much support from non-Jewish friends who are married to Jewish men and my Jewish friends; they have been helpful in offering their insights and wisdom.

I was surprised that I found studying in these small classes, which were academically rich and substantive, so much fun. In fact, I found Judaism so accessible that

I wanted to learn more; we decided to take more private classes with Rabbi Weiss. I expected to learn a lot about Judaism but did not expect to learn so much about Aaron and myself. Experiencing this process together has made us even stronger, for which I will always be grateful.

I am so grateful to Rabbi Weiss for her guidance, nurturing, and assistance at every stage of the conversion process. Her approach to teaching and basing her lessons in both history and contemporary life has given me a well-rounded, fresh perspective on Judaism that offers practical implications for day-to-day life. While I truly miss our mornings talking with Rabbi Weiss, I am very proud to have converted to Judaism.

Aaron's Perspective On Studying Judaism

Aaron: I had dated a few other non-Jewish women before Ahava, but none of those relationships were serious enough that I wanted to talk about them with my parents. When I told them about Ahava, my parents told me, "As long as you're happy, that's all that matters." I also had a cousin who had married someone who wasn't Jewish and it wasn't an issue for our family.

Studying alongside Ahava and learning from Rabbi Weiss has been so intellectually appealing; as an adult, I have learned to appreciate stories from the Torah that I learned as a young child in what might be called a "sugar-coated" version. Rabbi Weiss's classes were a great connection to my earlier studies and learning. I hadn't had any formal Jewish education since I was fifteen years old, so it was meaningful and interesting to explore and study Judaism as an adult.

When I was in London during my junior year of college, a group of Jewish friends and I spent a week in Venice. We were invited to a *Shabbat* (the Jewish Sabbath) service and lunch afterward at an Orthodox synagogue—where men and women sat separately—in the Jewish quarter of Venice. We also went to St. Peter's Cathedral in Rome, where my friends went to confession. The experiences there really helped reinforce for me the connections between Judaism and Catholicism.

Ahava Finds Judaism a Better Fit

Ahava: One especially appealing aspect of Judaism for me is the value and focus on family and community. As a people, Jews have had to overcome so many obstacles to survive. As a result, I believe there is a deep commitment to remember and honor their history to help prevent similar outcomes.

Growing up in the Catholic Church, I heard so much about heaven and hell. In the year that I studied Judaism, we barely discussed the afterlife. When we did, it was never a focal point. I love Judaism's focus on life, not the afterlife. If you approach life with the idea that you have just one shot at "getting it right," I think you set yourself up for more happiness and success.

I struggled with other aspects of Catholicism as well. I think that Jesus was an amazing, selfless person who set a strong foundation for teaching the value of charity, community, and sacrifice; however, I struggled with the idea that he was God's son who had risen from the dead. I also disagree with the Church's stance on homosexuals, gay marriage, divorce, and even abortion; Judaism is more accepting of these issues. I was relieved to find out that many rabbis are willing to officiate at gay marriages. I learned that if a woman's life is at risk, she is not merely allowed but encouraged to have an abortion.

I like Judaism's approach to confession and forgiveness, which I think makes people more accountable and conscious of their actions and how they affect other people. The concept of confessing once a year—at Yom Kippur—and to seek forgiveness first from individuals you have wronged and only then from God is more appealing to me than the concept of a weekly confessional, as is the case in the Catholic Church

I value Judaism's appreciation for women, whose strong stories are beautifully depicted in the Bible, and how women can be rabbis in Conservative and Reform Judaism.

I also appreciate that Judaism has a much stronger focus on study and learning than does Catholicism—the Jews study history, arts, ancestry, music, law, and the Bible. When I first started my classes in Judaism, I told my mom how little I remembered from the Bible even though I'd attended four years of Catholic school and later Catholic religious school classes. I assumed that I'd read the Bible and that I just had a terrible memory for it, but my mother told me that I probably had never read the Bible during those school years. From my perspective, education is so important on so many levels and I love that Judaism puts such high values on education, both secular and sacred.

Now that I've converted, we have *mezuzot* (the plural of *mezuzah*, which is the prayer scroll in a small, decorative fixture affixed to the doorways of Jewish homes) throughout our apartment. Although I'd never seen or even heard of them until I met Aaron, the *mezuzot* offer me a warm sense of welcome and security.

We also have hosted and attended several *Shabbat* dinners with our Jewish and non-Jewish friends. I have been overwhelmed with the support I've received about my decision to convert from our friends and family members. For a lot of our friends—those who are Jewish, those who aren't, and those who are in interfaith relationships—my process has been a learning experience for them as well. It's been a table-turning experience, as I can now teach Jewish-born friends about Judaism! Hosting these dinners has just been purely delightful. What's better than cooking, talking, and spending a night surrounded with friends?

Ahava's Food, Glorious Food

Ahava: We also hosted a Hanukkah dinner in December 2012; we used readings for all eight days of

Hanukkah that Rabbi Weiss had given us. Although some of our guests weren't Jewish and others weren't particularly religious, I wasn't sure how asking everyone to read something would be received. I am happy to report that everyone really enjoyed it. I've been surprised by the nostalgia many people feel when they participate in these traditions, many of which they've ignored for years. We've celebrated Rosh Hashanah for the past two years with a local friend, who typically invites more than thirty people to her home each year. We are already anticipating celebrating the Jewish New Year with our friend and her friends again next year. As some of my best childhood memories are from our family's Thanksgiving and Christmas dinners, I look forward to introducing my immediate family to our Jewish holidays and traditions. Shared meals and cooking together were an integral part of our family's history; it's not a surprise, then, that I am enjoying learning how to make traditional Jewish foods. It's been great; Aaron's father is Ashkenazic and his mom is Sephardic, so I've learned the different ways to prepare certain holiday foods, like Passover's *haroset* (symbolic—and delicious—dish, often made with apples, nuts, and honey). *Challah* (a sweet, braided bread often served at *Shabbat* dinners and special holiday meals) and honey is definitely one of my favorite snacks.

If you had predicted that Aaron and I would find ourselves in a synagogue on a weeknight to watch—and laugh hysterically—at a children's Purim production at a synagogue, I never would have believed you, but that happened! The kids were great and we enjoyed ourselves immensely. I don't think the kids even realized how much they were learning during the Purim celebration because they were having so much fun. Our classes also opened many doors for us and introduced us to Jewish communal activities.

Ahava Identifies as a Jewish Person Couple Practices Tzedakah

Ahava: Some time ago, I asked Aaron when he thought I might "feel" Jewish; I wasn't sure if or when I would ever feel Jewish, especially because I had never before identified strongly with a religion. Then, a few months ago, when I was talking to someone, I said "we" when I was talking about Jewish people. Initially, I didn't notice, but then it struck me. Honestly, I am not wholly sure what changed or when it did, but I now identify with the Jewish people. I think that sense of identification comes from Jewish people's strong sense of community, locally, nationally, and around the world. Even before Aaron and I married, his mother made me a lifetime Hadassah (American Jewish women's volunteer organization) member; I now receive their newsletters, which highlight Hadassah's remarkable efforts around *tikkun olam* (healing or repairing the world through good acts or good deeds).

I grew up practicing *tikkun olam* and *tzedakah* (to perform acts of charity or donate money), although our Catholic family didn't know those words. I grew up in a family that felt very strongly about charity. Our parents taught us that charity isn't just about giving money. In many ways, giving time and effort is more valuable than money. Years ago, my dad organized a food drive through his work, and they have raised tons of food for shelters every year. I hope to live up to his example and instill a feeling of obligation in our children about helping other people. I also want to teach them how rewarding it is to help others. I also look forward to learning more with our children, when we have them, and sharing our Jewish traditions and holidays with them.

We very much hope and pray that we will be blessed with children; we will raise them in *shalom bay'yit* (a peaceful home). We will join a synagogue where we will attend services and get involved in the community's activities. Our children will attend Hebrew school and, we hope, celebrate becoming a *bar* or *bat mitzvah*.

Several times a year, Aaron and I evaluate what we have and donate what we don't need. We also put spare change in our *tzedakah* box. At the end of the year, we will donate the money to cancer research, which is something important to us both.

CHAPTER SIX

African-American Woman Humbled to Call Herself Jewish

*Committed to Social Justice:
Insatiable Thirst for Jewish Knowledge
Drives Woman to Pursue Her Dream*

A middle-aged African-American dynamo, Ruth's energy, passion, and enthusiasm for social justice and Judaism inspire others to follow her lead. A high school dropout by choice, Ruth was a student of the streets who collaborated first with other anti-Vietnam War protesters, many of them Jewish, and later, fellow labor organizers. Throughout several careers—political activist, artist, teacher, and labor organizer—Ruth has worked to make a positive difference in the lives of the young, the disenfranchised, and the powerless. Teaching Ruth about Judaism was a remarkable opportunity for me, as her thirst for more reading assignments was nearly unquenchable. She pushed me to create an even more expansive reading list than many of my students had.

Ruth's Exodus

Ruth: I am the granddaughter of sharecroppers. My maternal grandmother was determined to see all of her children raised and educated north of the Mason-Dixon line, although they were born in the South. She knew that if her seven daughters and one son remained in the South, their prospects for advancement and a good life were grim; even service jobs in the North before and during World War II offered opportunities to African-Americans that weren't available in the South. Although my grandmother was Pentecostal, she departed from the religious practice of dressing modestly. "God created my elbows," she would tell me. "There's no reason for people not to see them." She also told me that Jesus was fine, but there was God before Jesus. Unusual, too, in wanting her daughters to delay marriage and childbearing, my grandmother wanted them to first know how to read and make their way in the world.

After he was stabbed over a card game, my maternal grandfather "found God" and became an itinerant

Pentecostal minister. Preferring small storefront congregations, my grandfather was often unemployed and financially unstable. Nevertheless, because he preached before other religious congregations and knew other faith leaders, including rabbis, who came to their home, his family life was rich and diverse.

My first clear recollections of family life in Washington, DC, where we moved when I was four, was going to a newly-integrated elementary school, populated predominantly by African-American and Jewish students. Someone had set fire to the front door of the school as a protest against us, the African-American students. I remember feeling very nervous about the situation, but no one explained what had happened. My neighborhood was filled with African-American, Jewish, Polish, and Italian families, and the kids all played together. When the Jewish kids avoided groups of Polish and Italian kids to avoid getting beaten up, my mother cautioned me against getting involved or picking sides. I also remember my mother taking me to Martin Luther King's "I Have a Dream" speech at the Lincoln Memorial during the March on Washington. I was all dressed up but overwhelmed by the sea of people and wanted to stay away from the crowds.

Because our school had so many Jewish students and Jewish teachers, we had days off for the Jewish holidays and we learned Jewish customs, rituals, and songs. Even after all these years, I still have the clay *menorah* (candlestick holder used in Jewish worship that holds seven candles) I made in school somewhere. Even with that

Jewish influence, most of my childhood was spent in the Pentecostal Church. My mother, like her mother, was a more modern Pentecostal; she believed that my older sister and I should have experiences outside of church and dress more contemporarily than traditional Pentecostal women did. Everything in moderation was her approach; as a result, we had experiences that my cousins, who went to church every day, didn't. My mother felt that giving us a good foundation was key and that we would find our way back to what we needed religiously. She wanted us to be exposed to the larger world, as she wasn't given those opportunities as a young girl.

When we traveled to New York City to see relatives, my father always reminded us that there would be no place for us to stop and use a bathroom until we got to New Jersey. As an African-American family traveling through Washington, DC, Maryland, and Delaware in the late 1950s and early 1960s, it wasn't so easy for us since there were no places along the highway at which we could stop to use the restrooms. When my father stopped at a highway gas station to get gas, everyone else stayed in the car. We never traveled to the South to visit relatives. In fact, I never went to any Southern states until I was working as an organizer when I was in my forties!

My parents split up when I was very young, and my sister and I lived with my mother. Although my father liked the idea of having children, the reality was different for him. Since he hadn't been nurtured as a child and was raised by distant relatives, he didn't know how to be a father. My father, who never had the chance to have a childhood, was very self-centered.

Since my mother had to work and care for two young girls on her own, religion became less of a constant presence in her life. She abandoned the pretense of being a long-suffering Christian wife and focused on creating a life that she could afford. After my parents divorced, my father was in his own world in a religious frenzy; I saw him when we celebrated our birthdays together, as we had birthdays just days apart. When I was young, we'd talk on the phone every day, but as I became a teenager, we drifted further apart.

Leaving the Church
Leaving School

Ruth: By the time I became a teenager, I'd left the church. My mother made one last-ditch effort with me when she arranged to have me baptized at age twelve. Let me tell you, being immersed in ice cold water, not once, but twice, is a very different experience than going to the *mikveh* (bath used for the purpose of ritual immersion) where you're cradled in God's hands.

I dropped out of high school when I was in ninth grade. I found my "education" in politics and demonstrations and teach-ins. I connected with a group of students and teachers to create a makeshift school. I took classes, taught, and ran a day-care center for children of protesters. We even had an overnight shelter for the kids whose parents got arrested during protests.

Those were great teenage years where I learned so much. I felt the world was passing me by in school. If I didn't get out and into the fray, I feared that I'd always be playing catch-up and would forever be left behind. Almost all my fellow anti-Vietnam War protesters were Jewish. They were the new Jewish left. No one was religious, but they were highly political. I was gassed at the Pentagon and at the FBI headquarters and I got knocked around a bit, but I never got arrested. In the African-American community, getting arrested was not OK. My parents were civil servants, and I knew I had to protect them and other relatives from that. There was too much at stake, so I stayed on the right side of the law.

Some time later—and without a high school diploma or a GED—I entered art school at the Corcoran School of Art as a painting student. I loved every minute of my experience there; it was a creative and yeasty time for students and instructors. Although the school had very few Jews enrolled then, I developed friendships with other art students and maintained my friendships with the Jewish activists from my days protesting.

As a preschool teacher in a Quaker school in the mid-1980s, I incorporated a lot of Jewish cultural practices and holidays into my curriculum. So many of the Jewish families there knew nothing about Hanukkah or other Jewish holidays.

I segued from political activism and teaching into labor organizing, which I did during the 1990s. I wanted to change and transform lives. I loved barnstorming the country and helping union campaigns.

Caring for an Ill Relative
Leads to the Study of Judaism

Ruth: When my mother, who has since died, became ill, I returned to Washington, DC, and did more work in social justice. When my mother went into renal failure, I began taking her to her dialysis treatments, which she'd undergone for many years, at a location not far from Sixth and I, a synagogue in downtown Washington, DC. Watching my mother dwindle and shrink into herself after being so robust and vibrant was painful to observe. One day, an e-mail sent to me had a live link to Rabbi Weiss's class Basic Judaism for Jews and Non-Jews Alike and preparations for conversions. I clicked on the link and thought, "Whoa, what's this? Conversions?" The testimonials from former students were compelling, so I signed up for her class. It was perfect because I could drop my mother off for her dialysis and take Rabbi Weiss's class. It was *beshert* (meant to be). I'm reading passages from Genesis in the Hebrew Bible—the same passages I read as a child—and people are asking questions. I asked Rabbi Weiss, "Are we supposed to ask questions?" Little did I know then that that's what Jews do—question, probe, debate! It's so different than in the Christian church, where asking questions is not acceptable. If we asked questions in the Pentecostal Church, people believed that Satan was testing our commitment to God and religion.

During the introductory class, I didn't consider

converting to Judaism at all. I was learning and reading. We got more books at every class, and I would stay up all night reading some of the books, especially books by Joseph Telushkin. I would tell Rabbi Weiss, "I'm out of reading material, and I want more." Then I began to buy books on my own. Absorbing all this information brought out the "nerd" in me: I love to think, write, analyze, and read. Christianity never offered me a place for questions, for intellect, or to be cerebral.

I didn't want to stop my individual study, which had lots of homework and reading, but my mother experienced a series of medical crises. Because she was so ill and struggling to prepare herself to die, I chose not to tell her about my studying Judaism. Fearing that I would simply drift religiously, she urged me to get back to church to find Jesus. I was shoved out her room and into the hospital corridor when she had a heart attack; I remember I stood by myself and said, "*Hineni*" (Here I am, God). That was when I believe I took my first beginning steps to becoming a Jew. When my mother was dying, I had a heightened awareness of everything, including all the changes happening to me internally through my spiritual awakening. After I came out of the *mikveh* and held the Torah and signed the pledge, I thought to myself, "What now? What do I do now? I don't have to study?"

My Jewish friends and I went out for Chinese food and to talk about my experience—it was my own version of a *bat mitzvah* (the coming-of-age ritual Jewish girls experience at twelve or thirteen years old) party. After that, I started making Jewish choices, including "outing" myself as a Jew at work. That way, I could celebrate the Jewish holidays rather than clandestinely take time off from work. I began to create a Jewish identity, which fascinated some people. I was fortunate that when I converted in July 2009, my workplace was extremely culturally diverse and that diversity was highly respected.

Judaism was a place of refuge for me at that time; my mother had been the family matriarch and with her death, my family was out of control. My relatives were 110 percent over the top about Jesus and my mother's reconciling in heaven with Jesus. My older sister had been a full-blown Buddhist since sixteen. Reading about Jewish observances of death and mourning really helped me; I had something to hold onto with that reading.

After hearing me explain that I was Jewish, one aunt said, "You could be a Jew for Jesus." She told me that, with my decision to be Jewish, I couldn't be in heaven with the rest of our family. My mother was dying as my aunt claimed that she was glad that my mother would never know that I couldn't accept Christ into my heart. It was strange; at one moment, she was my aunt and the next moment, she was an anti-Semite. Since my mother's funeral, I've not spoken to her, and I don't believe we'll ever talk again.

Friendships End
Friendships Develop

Ruth: I'm very supportive of Israel, though I've not visited yet. I hope to travel around Israel for several weeks—perhaps next fall—so I can really see the country and get to know the people. By virtue of my conversion, several of my long-term friendships ended. There was simply no middle ground about these individuals' left-wing views on Israel. I still have tremendous respect for these individuals and the social justice work they do. Most of my social and political activism was never tethered to a state, yet now I have this connection to Israel.

My sister and I talk about our respective religious journeys, and I attended a confirmation ceremony for her at her Buddhist temple. Now working as a lay leader in her Buddhist temple, she came to my conversion ceremony and has attended my Passover Seders (the Passover ritual meal to observe the liberation of the Jews after being exiled from Egypt and wandering in the desert for forty years; Seder means "order" as there is a precise order of the readings that are recited before and after the holiday meal). She's encouraged me to get my dining room in order so that we can have a proper *Seder* at my home. We really haven't gone that far afield religiously from our religious roots; my mother raised us to land wherever we needed to be and to look for opportunities. When I look back, there were a lot of negatives for me about my Pentecostal experiences, but they gave me the knowledge that belonging can be a good thing. They made me comfortable with religious communities and religiosity. Some Jewish-born people often struggle with the Liturgy (religious service) and Orthodox Judaism. I'm leaning toward finding a Conservative synagogue, as I feel most at home there, though I've experienced both

Reform and Orthodox services.

Some of my friends have noticed a change in me since my conversion. They say that I am a better person now, more whole and absent a sense of struggle and brokenness. I don't know if I have "gelled," as some suggested, but in being Jewish, I have found the roots of all that I value: justice, fighting for equity, belonging to a group of people whether you like them or not, doing the right thing, etc. I fought for all those things.

Through my religious studies, I found the roots and antecedents and people who shaped those ideas and values; that's made me feel far more rooted and grounded. I understand what it means to repair the world. I had never had a religious or spiritual root, but now I have ideological, political, and spiritual roots. I am much calmer now. Judaism has made it clear to me that change comes in different forms. If you don't have radical change, organic change can be equally powerful. Judaism has helped me appreciate the human scale of change: changing hearts and minds.

After all these years, I am both humbled and grateful to be Jewish.

CHAPTER SEVEN

Christian Woman Pursues Long-Held Dream and Converts to Judaism

Post-Divorce: Woman Decides to Act on Her Own Needs and Desires

When Alanna first walked into my office, I wondered why she was coming to see me—she seemed wholly self-assured and confident, not on a path of searching for anything, much less converting to Judaism. Soon after she began talking, I was drawn to her warmth and her beautiful smile; her determination to study Judaism with the objective to be a part of the Jewish people became crystal clear. Given her desire and determination, I told her, "We will begin our studies and see where the road will take us. Let the journey begin."

Bright, articulate, and a powerhouse at the law firm she manages, Alanna is not married to anyone of the Jewish faith and she is not raising her children as Jews because she shares custody with her non-Jewish ex-husband. Growing up in a very conservative Christian home in the South, Alanna always felt out of place and uncomfortable with Christian pedagogy that quashed questioning. She ventured into more diverse environments with her high school theater group and later while attending the University of Miami, where Judaism continued to beckon to her. Reluctant to disrupt or upset her parents, with whom she is very close, Alanna deferred her desire to study and convert to Judaism for many years. It wasn't until she ended her marriage that she felt ready to do something for and by herself. Intelligent and articulate, energetic and driven, Alanna is now pursuing an Orthodox conversion, after having gone through conversion within Conservative Judaism. Her decision to become an Orthodox Jew entails a journey that I could never have predicted!

Alanna's Youth

Alanna: As a child, I enjoyed the social aspects of church and church-related camps, but I always struggled with Christian ideology and the idea that Jesus was the son of God. My parents, who possess a tremendous and vigorous love of Christianity, were very involved with the Presbyterian Church. In our church, once a question was answered, we were supposed to believe in that answer, no questions asked; no deeper inquiry was allowed. The idea that I should simply accept what the Bible said was soul crushing, and I couldn't accept the idea that we are all born sinners, as Christianity states.

I grew up in a very comfortable home in a small town in western North Carolina. My father was a bank executive and my mother worked occasionally as a substitute teacher. I have one older brother who has remained in that small town, to this day. When I was young, our family attended church no fewer than three times each week and had Bible study every morning at breakfast. I also attended a parochial elementary school.

Because I asked questions and expressed concerns about Christian ideologies—when those were neither encouraged nor allowed in our devout environment—I felt like an outsider in my own family. I deeply admired my parents and their abiding faith, but I knew from a fairly young age that I couldn't be an observant Christian when I no longer lived at home.

Burgeoning Exposures to Judaism

Alanna: When I entered high school, my very cloistered world began to expand. I became very involved in acting in several venues: at my high school, in a statewide summer youth program, and with a community theater club for youth. Through these activities, including a theater-based trip to New York City, I was introduced to a wider and more diverse array of youth, including some who were Jewish. I give my parents a great deal of credit, as they were very supportive of my interest in theater and in attending college far from our small town; they simply wanted me to be happy.

Once I was at the University of Miami in Miami, Florida, I became very exposed to Judaism. My room-mate, who became my best friend, was Jewish, as were many of my friends. I wasn't merely exposed to Jewish people; I was exposed to the community and spiritu-ality of Judaism. I was deeply moved by and drawn to my friends' Jewish traditions and customs. I lit my very first menorah (candlestick holder used in Jewish worship that holds seven candles) with my roommate and listened to her recite the Hanukkah blessings; in time, I learned those blessings. I was struggling with conflicting desires: I so much wanted to learn more about Judaism and embrace it as my own religion, yet I also wanted to avoid upsetting or angering my devout Christian parents.

In my youthful naiveté, I thought that if I found someone Jewish to marry, my parents could understand my decision to convert to Judaism if it was for love! As the old expression goes, "Man plans, God laughs." While I dated some lovely young men who were Jewish, I ultimately married a Catholic man who didn't prac-tice his religion. Given all that, I decided to put aside my thoughts of converting to Judaism, figuring it was simply a youthful folly.

Marriage, Motherhood, and Religion

Alanna: After our marriage in 1999 and the births of our children—our daughter in 2000 and our son in 2008—we had a completely secular home. We did celebrate Christmas and Easter, though in a purely secular fashion. For me, Easter wasn't about Christ rising from the dead; rather, it was about buying fun Easter baskets for my children, dressing up in fancy clothes, and hiding eggs.

In an effort to replicate for my children my childhood sense of belonging to something larger than myself—even though I ultimately left that community—my husband and I attended a few churches. Feeling no connection with or pull toward any of those churches, we eventually abandoned the idea of joining a Christian community. My interest in Judaism had not waned throughout my marriage, though I didn't pursue the idea of conversion during those years.

After the birth of our son, I felt that things weren't right in my life. Neither a career change nor our move to the greater Washington, DC, area filled the emptiness I felt. I was eager to develop my own identity, not just the identity of someone's wife and someone's mother. Although my then husband and I were—and remain—good friends, our marriage had been unhappy for years; we divorced in August 2012. After our separation, the idea of converting pulled at me once again.

Divorce and JDate

Alanna: When I was ready to begin dating about six months or so after the divorce, I knew I wanted to date Jewish men, so I signed up with JDate.com. With one Jewish man, there was an instant "boom" and sense of connection, although the relationship ended badly after several months. Dating him sparked my desire to start investigating conversion. Sometimes it's difficult for me to articulate, but when people around me discuss Judaism, they're discussing something that feels as if it's been a part of me forever. I feel at home there. I feel so comfortable—almost on a cellular level—when I am with other Jewish people.

As I started reading other individuals' stories of conversion online, I learned about Rabbi Weiss and her first book, *Converting to Judaism: Choosing to be Chosen: Personal Stories*. Before our first meeting, I still wasn't sure I wanted to convert. As soon as I met her, however, I was absolutely sure of my desire, and no longer felt hesitant. I was no longer plagued by "what ifs?" and realized that it was time for me to do what was right for me, even if it wasn't right for my parents or others in my life. I don't ever want to dishonor or displease my parents, who have been nothing but loving and supportive role models for me. At the same time, I knew with complete certainty that my life would never be fulfilled and complete if I was not a Jew. It is simply who I am. I can never be anything else.

Unlike the Christian viewpoint that humans are born

sinners, the Jewish belief that we are all born good and that we have free will to do good or do evil resonates with me. I could never accept the concept of Jesus Christ as the Messiah, though I still struggle with the question of knowing when the Messiah will come. Judaism accepts my questions and encourages me to dig deeper to find the answers that are right for me. I absolutely love that about Judaism. I can stretch my intellect twenty-four hours a day, seven days a week and still have questions. My whole world has opened up, surrounded as I am by brilliant people who seek to question and think. It is empowering, yet humbling. God is good.

After my studies with Rabbi Weiss and my Conservative conversion, I found an Orthodox rabbi in Washington, DC, with whom I wanted to study. The opportunity to continue to question, question, and question again has been immensely rewarding and gratifying.

I regularly attend *Shabbat* (the Jewish Sabbath) services at two Orthodox *shuls* (synagogues)—one in the Washington, DC, area and one in western Maryland in the town where my boyfriend lives. He is an Orthodox Jewish man who is a widower and the father of a young boy. Will we marry one day? I don't know, though the relationship is very warm and loving now. His son is extremely observant and mine is completely secular. Our households are very different, although both are kosher! I participate in Torah study with the rabbi at my boyfriend's synagogue and in women's study groups as well, which I find very helpful and informative. They have been welcoming to me; I feel like they are "my people."

Creating a Jewish Home

Alanna: Although it's not always easy, I am *shomer Shabbas* (honoring the commandment to spend *Shabbat* in prayer, study, and communal Jewish life, rather than spending money, driving, or engaging in other commercial activities). It's such a small thing for God to ask us to do, given how much God gives us. I get excited for *Shabbat* every weekend; as late Friday afternoon arrives, I prepare for *Shabbat* by getting my home and myself ready for the holiday. It's a very peaceful and beautiful twenty-four hours, whether my children are with me or with their father. While they sometimes ask me, "Why can't you drive me . . . ," I do let them use their iPads, for example, as that doesn't impact my observation of the holiday. It is difficult, though, for my daughter who's now a traveling soccer superstar. When her games are on Sundays, it's no problem for me to come and cheer her on, but when they are on Saturdays—as my son's soccer games are—I will miss them, unless they are somewhere within walking distance of my home. This may be a difficult thing for my children to accept; otherwise, they are OK with my observances, even though they don't understand them.

Frankly, I was terrified to tell my parents about my decision to convert to Judaism. Because my parents are so enmeshed in Christianity and because I always made my parents proud, I really feared their reactions. After sweating bullets about telling them during a recent visit with them, it turned out to be fine. While my father wasn't excited about my decision, my mother said, "I am so glad you have found something. . . . You have been so empty for so long."

I'm looking forward with eagerness to celebrate the High Holidays this year. In fact, as office administrator for an international law firm, I have already prepped my senior staff members to be ready to fill in for me, during the several days I won't be in the office during Rosh Hashanah, Yom Kippur, Sukkot, and Simchat Torah.

My Journey of Judaism

Alanna: I haven't visited Israel yet, but I hope to go there in the next year or two. It's hard for me to envision myself living somewhere other than the United States, especially somewhere that I've yet to visit, but I believe it's my obligation to support those who want to make *aliyah* (moving to Israel).

Even now, I can't say I feel 100 percent Jewish, as I have so much still to learn. I'm on a journey. Rabbi Weiss has taught me so much: the traditions of Judaism, the holidays, the sense of community, and the *mitzvot* (plural of *mitzvah*, which means "commandment or obligation under Jewish law) of Judaism. I have learned that Judaism is about being loving to our fellow Jews, embracing them, praying with them, learning with them, and providing *tzedakah* (to perform acts of charity or donate money) in any way possible. I am so eager to learn what God has in store for me as I follow this sacred path to living a full life as an Orthodox Jewish woman.

I was always searching, always seeking something, and now I have found what I sought for so many years. I am so grateful to be studying and learning with so many people who are committed to their Judaism, especially Rabbi Weiss, who helped me get started on this journey.

CHAPTER EIGHT

Orthodox Jewish Woman & Blond-Haired, Blue-Eyed, Southern Christian Fall in Love

Two Lawyers of Divergent Backgrounds Find Bliss in Marriage, Judaism, and Family

Recently married, Ben and Sarah share a profession and now a religion, as Ben converted to Judaism shortly before the couple married. They live in the greater Washington, DC, area, and both work as attorneys. They met while Sarah, raised as an Orthodox Jew, was in law school. At the time of their interview, they had been married for one month. In a later conversation with the happily married couple, they announced the news that they had welcomed a baby daughter into their Jewish family.

It's clear that creating a loving, welcoming Jewish home is of paramount importance to the couple. Their goals are clearly defined: They speak of their desire to join and participate in a synagogue, send their children to religious and Hebrew school, establish family traditions of Hanukkah parties and Passover *Seders* (the Passover ritual meal to observe the liberation of the Jews after being exiled from Egypt and wandering in the desert for forty years. Seder means "order" as there is a precise order of the readings that are recited before and after the holiday meal), and celebrate *Shabbat* (the Jewish Sabbath). Family matters to both Ben and Sarah; Sarah's mother, who knew that Sarah had dated other non-Jewish men, supported her decision to marry Ben. Ben's mother was so enthusiastic about his decision to marry Sarah and convert to Judaism that she inquired whether she, too, should convert to Judaism.

After her parents divorced when she was fairly young, Sarah and her mother moved—both geographically and spiritually—from her highly Orthodox New York-based family. Judaism remained important to her, but neither she nor her mother adhered to Jewish traditions and practices with the same intensity then that they had during their time in New York.

Ben's frustrations with and alienation from many

Christian practices and beliefs began when he was young. Not only did he dislike the concept of spiritual authorities—the Pope, pastors, imams, etc.—Ben found the radical anti-science, anti-progress, and anti-tolerance practices of some Southern Christians wholly unacceptable. His exposure to Judaism in high school and college deepened his knowledge of and appreciation for Judaism, Jewish spirituality, and Jewish history. Even before meeting Sarah, he felt that the "essential building blocks to Judaism were already in place." Marrying Sarah, he explained, was the last catalyst Ben needed to begin his formal study of Judaism.

Ben's Movement From Christianity

Ben: Although I was born in Yugoslavia, I am quite Southern. For all practical purposes, I am from Augusta, Georgia, a typical Southern conservative Christian town, and a diehard Republican. When I was growing up, all my friends were very conservative Christians except for a couple of Jewish kids in school.

As I told the rabbis at the *beit din* (rabbinical court of Jewish laws), my interest in Judaism was due to a movement away from Christianity, which, for me, was so stifling intellectually and emotionally. There's lots of hypocrisy in the South; the church will preach one thing about what Jesus Christ said, which was a repetition from the Torah, and the moment you leave the church, those values go out the window. My first brush with Jewish spirituality was an Advanced Placement literature paper I wrote in my senior year of high school on Martin Buber and his book *I and Thou*. I was deeply impressed by Buber's idea that a purported atheist staring out his attic window is closer to God than the most ritual-observing priest. Later, I recently learned that this is closely related to *kavanah* (holy intention), which is one of my favorite Jewish concepts. That was the first time I began to feel that my spirituality was not inconsistent with my intellectualism or progressivism.

In college and law school, I told people I was an atheist, but I was never 100 percent comfortable with that. When I was growing up, we didn't go to church very often, although I went to Bible school on vacation and to summer camp with my Methodist friends. I was baptized as an Episcopalian. Denominations didn't mean that much then, as long as you were Protestant!

Sarah's Younger Years

Sarah: My family was very Orthodox, and all my early memories had to do with *Shabbat* and Jewish holidays. My grandparents were Holocaust survivors, and I had friends whose grandparents were also survivors. We all went to the same school and the same camp; Judaism was everywhere and everything. People who made it out of the Holocaust became atheists or very religious; we were very religious.

When we lived in New York—where my mother's

family was from—Orthodox Judaism guided every aspect of our lives. But when we lived in Florida, my mom was less religious. It was just my mom and me, and I think she felt that Orthodox Judaism was stifling; I felt it was stifling, too. My mom was a public school teacher, and her friends weren't all Jewish. We weren't closed off from the larger community.

Some of the good memories from that time are, of course, my friendships. My best friends now are from that time . . . when I went to Beth Shalom Academy. I hated going to religious school; now, I can appreciate it and, in fact, I can still speak Hebrew.

Ben's Family
Reactions and Responses

Ben: Being Christian was never very important to my parents, although I remember one funny incident when I was a teenager. When I went to get my driver's license, my father brought my baptismal certificate with us in case I had to prove I was Christian.

My dad, who was from the rural South, was brought up as a Southern Baptist. He used to teach Sunday school. When I would share a story from my studies with Rabbi Weiss, he'd say, "Oh yeah, I remember that story . . ." I think he believes in God a little bit, but he doesn't believe in the institution. Going to church was never a priority. Being Christian was never a priority, though we celebrated Christmas. My dad's sisters and his mother, who prayed for our souls, always wanted us to be more observant. However, they didn't shame us, and they were as nonjudgmental as you can be.

When I told my mother I was converting and explained why, her first question was, "Should I convert too?" They loved Sarah and there was no awkwardness. They liked Rabbi Weiss, too.

I've noticed that since we've begun going to services and studying, Sarah has come across the old songs and prayers that seemed very familiar to her. They remind her of her family.

No Need to Tell the World of His Judaism

Ben: During the conversion process, I wondered if Jewish people would accept me; for better or worse, many Jews have an "us versus them" mentality. With my blond hair and blue eyes and no Jewish ancestry, I worried that I wouldn't be accepted. I have found, though, that the vast majority of Jews I have met have gladly welcomed me to the community.

I also didn't understand that race and religion are identical in Judaism; later, I came to appreciate the concept of the nation of Israel. You can be born into the religion or join it; I learned from Rabbi Weiss that it's accepting Jewish traditions that makes someone a Jew. Judaism has never given me pause, but there's plenty about Jews that has—I have trouble with the people who grew up Jewish but never read critically the books of the Torah. As for the actual teachings and observances, I am sure that if I were in an Orthodox community, there are things I would reject. I do what I can; if we want to get to temple for *Shabbat* services, we have to get into the car and drive. A lot of people understand the need for flexibility. As for keeping kosher laws, we buy kosher food when we can, we observe what we can, but we can't afford to buy a whole new set of pots and pans. Sometimes we light candles and have a nice dinner at *Shabbat*; it doesn't feel like a religious ceremony but a nice family tradition. Jewish traditions are healthy, I think.

I don't walk around congratulating myself that I am now Jewish; it's not relevant to my life on a day-to-day basis. It's a very private thing; I don't shake someone's hand and say, "I'm Ben and I'm a Jew." People don't need to know that about me. I am not proselytizing my Jewish identity; I don't need to be a lobbyist for Judaism in every encounter.

Sarah Searches for a Synagogue

Sarah: My journey is the same as others: You start out religious, leave it for awhile, and then, when you meet someone, the religion comes back. I think that's pretty typical; for me, it was fine. Of course, I had told my mom about Ben's conversion, and I had dated non-Jewish men before Ben; although, my extended family doesn't know that Ben converted to Judaism. My mother always said that everyone should do what they want as long as they don't interfere with others.

Our wedding ceremony was very Jewish and both of us loved it; we had no aspects of a Christian ceremony. Since Ben converted, there's nothing that's been a surprise or different from what I'd envisioned. We have *Shabbat* dinners; when we have kids, they will go to religious school and learn what I learned.

None of the synagogues we've looked at joining meet our needs yet, with respect to their distance from our home and the type of services they offer. We'll find something. We just have to have one. Although we initially considered a Conservative synagogue, one with some English and some Hebrew, we later chose Temple Sinai, a Reform synagogue that we like very much. We wanted a synagogue that has a large membership; one where we'd see members of the synagogue in other aspects of our lives—out in the community, at after-school events, etc. When I was sent to religious school, I never saw those individuals outside of school. At an Orthodox service, you'll see that the men are serious and the women are pushing baby carriages and there's a little bit of talking. Kids are running up to the *bimah* (platform or podium in a synagogue), and I love that. People are contemplative and enjoy the experience.

Politics Make Strange Bedfellows

Ben: The politics of Israel are really sticky for me. Israel is treated like this magic shibboleth (custom) where the person who screams the loudest wins elections! I am often accused of being too pro-Israel as the Likud party gets more and more conservative. We should all start at the same place—that the preservation of Israel is paramount. I think that fighting with every neighbor is bad. I don't feel at all apologetic for believing in Israel. Sarah is a little more conservative than I am about Israel.

I am concerned that the "us versus them" mentality is getting more and more crystallized with Orthodox rabbis attacking others. As Jews, we're supposed to value progressive and democratic practices; I worry about that not happening.

Sarah's Views on Moving to Israel

Sarah: I could make *aliyah* (moving to Israel); I have family there, including an uncle who was born in New York. If there were problems in Israel that had it calling on American Jews to come and help, we would go. But, as far as making *aliyah* without that situation, I don't think we'd go. We're comfortable being American Jews, and we're fortunate to live in the United States. It's very abstract, but if something horrible happened in Israel, we would go.

Our careers are going well here, and our families are here. We do want to visit as soon as we can get the money together. I did two high school programs there and Ben's never been.

Family and family traditions mean everything to us, and through Ben's conversion studies, I have grown closer to the Jewish traditions, customs, and songs that were

familiar touchstones of my childhood. Ben has been—
and is—an amazingly supportive partner in this process
and has fully embraced Judaism as his own. We are so
blessed to be able to experience this journey together as
new parents, and I know we both look forward to seeing
what the future holds for us.

CHAPTER NINE

A Decades-Long Journey to Living a Jewish Life

Learn What You Can and
Prepare for Surprises

Thirty-seven year old Chaya has embraced Judaism as a single woman. Bright and articulate, Chaya, is a world traveler who now works for the federal government in the Washington, DC, area. Her travels were more than geographic explorations, as she also journeyed down many roads over many years before finding her spiritual home in Judaism. Thoughtful and wise, mature beyond her years, Chaya immersed herself in learning Hebrew prayers, studying the Hebrew language, and enrolling in a wide array of programs and classes offered by Jewish organizations. Unlike so many of my students who choose Judaism because they have fallen in love with a Jewish partner, Chaya turned to Judaism wholly for herself— she has no partner or spouse whose Judaism inspired a conversion. Deeply committed to her Jewish faith, Chaya will only consider dating someone who is either Jewish or who would be willing to convert to Judaism. As she so poignantly states, "I'm not dating for fun [now]."

Chaya Speaks Her Mind

Chaya: Being a Jew makes sense for me; it connects with me in a way I had not connected with anything else. I've been at this—the process of embracing Judaism—for about seventeen years. Given that, I've had a lot of time to think about this. Judaism is the only thing that resonates for me, and it's the only thing that makes me feel grounded. It wasn't any one event that caused me to embrace Judaism; rather, it was a series of small encounters that caused me to lean in that direction.

I grew up as a Christian in both Pentecostal and Baptist churches. My mother and young brother have had their own spiritual journeys in the last several years. My mother and brother are now Buddhists. I, myself, dabbled in Buddhism when I was younger. My father doesn't care that I have left the Christian faith; as long as I'm happy, he's fine with whatever I choose.

Growing Up
Many Residences
Many Church Affiliations

Chaya: Although I was born in a small town in upstate New York in 1976, we moved a great deal when I was young, as my father worked as a librarian for the Veterans Administration. My mother, who had also been a librarian, stayed home to raise my younger brother and me. When I was born, I was baptized and given saints' names for my first and middle names. I also had godparents. My mother was raised as a Catholic, and I believe that my father had converted to Catholicism. Then, when we moved to California a few years after I was born, my parents became Protestant. I think there had been some problem or issue with the local parish priest. My brother, who was born in California, was not baptized. When I was four years old, we moved again, this time to Kansas. It's from there that I have my first memories of religion. I was baptized when I was seven years old with baptismal classes and the dip in the pool that was behind the church choir loft. Then, we moved to New York, and my parents stayed there. There was only one Jewish family in town, and their son, Sam, was in all my classes. The teachers always lined the students up, according to height, and the two of us, as the tallest, were always at the front of the line.

In sixth grade, when we had to do reports on different countries and bring in ethnic foods, Sam reported on

Israel and I think that his mother made latkes to bring to school. Around the same time, I was reading *The Hiding Place,* by Corrie ten Boom with John and Elizabeth Sherrill, about ten Boom's family who hid Jews in Holland, and *The Diary of Anne Frank*. Ten Boom's story was the other side of the Anne Frank story. I thought so much about their experiences when I was a young girl; I always wished I'd been there to help them. In my seventh grade English class, we read play version of *The Diary of Anne Frank*, and I read the part of Anne.

By the time I was in high school, where I was very active in theater, I'd "waved goodbye" to Christianity. In my senior year of high school, I played the role of the eldest daughter in *Fiddler on the Roof*, which, perhaps ironically, was my entry point into Judaism. Sam also had a role in the play, as did his younger sister who was only in middle school. Their mother invited all the cast members over for a *Shabbat* (the Jewish Sabbath) dinner and for a dinner and *havdalah* (the ceremony that signifies the end of *Shabbat*, after three stars can be seen in the Saturday evening sky) service. She demonstrated the *Shabbat* candle prayers and taught them to us for the play. I was hooked; I loved the whole idea of *Shabbat*. When I was growing up, I hated Sundays. After spending three hours in church, our family would then go out for doughnuts; to this day, I still don't like doughnuts! I had a visceral hate of the day, yet when I looked at the Jewish Sabbath experience, it was all about dinner and candles and peaceful quiet, which I loved.

The Pentecostal church my family attended in New

York never resonated with me at all. Every Sunday morning was a family battle: I didn't wear dresses, and I hated the junior congregation at church. I thought the guy who led it was a tyrant, and I simply didn't want anything to do with it. I'm not sure why my parents transitioned from attending a Baptist church to a Pentecostal church. Perhaps it was because the Pentecostal church was close to where we lived or maybe friends from my father's work encouraged them to attend. It was very strange. It was housed in what had been an old skating rink in what was once a train station. Now, it's probably one of those supersized churches with thousands of members. They attended this church in the mid-1980s, when people simply didn't go to church in roller skating rinks—it was simply too odd. At that church, there was a rock band and an electric piano; some members spoke in tongues. At first, hearing people speak in tongues freaked me out a bit. Later, it was simply disconcerting, and then it was just boring.

After we went there for a number of years, my family moved into town and attended a Baptist church that was a bit more mainstream and more comfortable. Then, when I was a high school freshman, they found yet another Pentecostal church. By then, I was done with religion; my parents would go to the adult congregational services and I would take off and walk three miles home. Sometime before that, my parents dragged me kicking and screaming to church on Saturday nights or Sunday mornings. My friends couldn't understand why we went to church services on Saturday nights. It made no sense to them, but it didn't strike me as strange until after I went to college.

When I attended college in New York, I began to recognize that Judaism and Baptism were not the same; as a child, I hadn't been aware of any real differences. I grew up knowing that some people went to church on Sunday and some went on Saturday, but that was about it. During college, I went through a couple of years of "detoxing from religion" so I could just focus on school. There had been some family tension around religion. I was furious that my parents stopped going to church after I went to college, yet they had forced me to go to religious services for so many years before that. I thought to myself, "Why did you stop after making me attend church? Why didn't my brother (then a high school freshman or sophomore) have to keep going to church?" It wasn't until I was a bit older that I realized that my parents may have had other reasons for stopping their church involvement: They might have grown tired of church politics, they might have decided that the ten years of religious education my brother and I received was sufficient, or they might have realized that church simply wasn't for them any longer. I understand that parents would want to inculcate their children with moral values—some of which were grounded in Bible stories and lessons; I was angry for a couple of years and then let it go.

I considered myself an outsider at the State University of New York (SUNY) campus I attended, as the student body was about half Jewish and half Catholic and came mostly from greater New York City. As someone who was neither Jewish nor Catholic and from the western part of New York, I felt as if they were speaking a completely foreign language. I quickly learned some *New Yorkese* and some Yiddish, so I spent my first couple of years assimilating. My first roommate was Jewish and I made a *menorah* (candlestick holder used in Jewish worship that holds seven candles) out of paper and paper flames. My roommate's *bubbie* (grandmother) and *zayde* (grandfather) were so impressed with my little paper *menorah* when they visited her. Her grandparents were so impressed that I knew the Hanukkah prayers and that I was encouraging their granddaughter to be more observant that they sent me care packages!

During my freshman year, I also joined the crew team; on spring break, we all went to train in Augusta, Georgia. One night, when two of my crewmates asked if anyone wanted to come with them to a synagogue, I said, "Yes, what's it for?" It turned out to be Purim that night, so my very first holiday experience in a synagogue was Purim, which was new and fun and exciting. My friends had given me a rundown of what to expect. I had a blast; some congregants invited us to come to their home for dinner, which we did.

I took Hebrew as a sophomore; and I began to explore Buddhism as a junior in college. That was around the same time that my mother looked into Buddhism for herself. Later that year, I simply began "religion shopping" by reading, reading, and reading. My answer to everything is to seek information from books; after all, my parents are both librarians. As a senior, I found a rabbi

and began going to a synagogue. I was working at the
student association center, so I knew people from all the
different campus groups. When a *Hillel* (a college-based
Jewish program) board member asked me if I wanted
to go to synagogue with him, I said, "Yes." We went to
a Conservative synagogue where he sat with me and
helped me with the prayers. I went to synagogue services
for about eight months and also began attending conversion classes. I was given a Torah and a prayer: "May you
live to be 120 years old."

After I started dating someone who wasn't Jewish, I
became consumed by horrible guilt, so I stopped conversion classes and stopped attending services. I was morti-
fied that I was dating someone not Jewish, even though
I, myself, wasn't officially Jewish. Looking back, I am not
sure why I was so ashamed, but at the time, it seemed so
logical. After all, I was only twenty-one. Now I wonder
why I simply didn't carry on and see what might have
happened. Although I'm sorry that I didn't continue my
studies toward conversion, in retrospect, it doesn't matter
all that much now.

After graduation, I began working as a commercial
banker and moved to Seattle, Washington, where I dated
a Jewish guy who I dragged to synagogue with me. It was
funny; we met on a hike and after I said something in
Yiddish, he said to me, "I fell in love with you right then.
You need to meet my mother!"

When I moved to Russia in 2003, it was simply
too dangerous to do anything Jewish there. It was bad
enough to be American; I didn't want to be targeted or

singled out for any other reason. During all my travels, I'd keep reading and keep thinking about elements of Judaism that I knew; I was aware of when Jewish holidays were, and I was thinking about which foods were kosher and which weren't. Whenever I had clam chowder, I'd think to myself, "This is *treyf* (food that isn't kosher) in the worst possible way," and I'd experience so much food guilt.

Once I returned to the United States, I attended graduate school in Northern California. I was invited to a Passover *Seder* (the Passover ritual meal to observe the liberation of the Jews after being exiled from Egypt and wandering in the desert for forty years. Seder means "order" as there is a precise order of the readings that are recited before and after the holiday meal). by a friend whose father was Jewish and whose mother was Catholic. Another guest—an Israeli man—and I got into a deep debate about the conversion process in general and, more specifically, women's role in the conversion process. Everyone else was simply speechless. Because I'd lived in a Buddhist monastery, I think people thought that I was Buddhist. It was that experience that made me realize I needed to go back to Judaism.

When I ended up living on the East Coast—in the Washington, DC, area—I attended services and other Jewish programs at Sixth and I, located only a few blocks away from my new home. Three weeks later, I called Rabbi Weiss, whom I had found online, and began my studies with her.

One positive aspect to my conversion being a long

and slow process—of seventeen years—is that I have much more perspective now than at twenty. Then, everything was black and white with no wiggle room; you're either dating a Jew or you're not. I think that's why I stopped my conversion studies. Twenty years later, I have a bit more perspective and appreciation for looking at things in a less regimented fashion. And, much has changed in fifteen years. When I went to a Conservative synagogue in Albany, New York, no women wore *tallitot* (prayer shawls) or *kippot* (head coverings). Yet the first time I showed up at a Conservative synagogue in Washington, DC, I thought to myself, "Whoa, why are so many women wearing *tallitot* and *kippot* and no one is even batting an eye? I didn't get that memo!"

In my studies, I've relearned some things I knew before, but I didn't know them the way I thought I knew them. For example, I had a twenty-year-old's understanding of the differences between Reform, Conservative, and Orthodox Jewry; I thought that virtually all Reform Jews ate bacon cheeseburgers, and I only went to the synagogue on Rosh Hashanah and Yom Kippur because of tradition. Now, however, I appreciate that someone can be a Reform Jew and an observant Jew. It's been a constant process of education and remaining open to hearing and learning about other Jews' views on different topics.

I've been participating in many minyanim (independent groups of Jews who meet for prayer, study, socializing, social action, etc.), and have created my own little Jewish world. Being a liberal Conservative Jew sounds like an oxymoron, but it's not. From a political standpoint, it's wholly confusing—how can someone be a liberal Conservative?—but religiously, it makes great sense for me. It's been interesting having conversations with my parents in which I explain that I'm Conservative, but not politically!

As a vegetarian, I find it easy enough to keep kosher at home. I haven't *kashered* (the process of making a space kosher) my kitchen yet, but I only buy fruits and vegetables and other foods that are *hekshered* (approved as kosher). I am not *shomer Shabbas* (honoring the commandment to spend Shabbat in prayer, study, and communal Jewish life, rather than spending money, driving, or engaging in other commercial activities), but I'm entertaining the idea; it's a process.

At this point, I've experienced the entire year of Jewish holidays. This year, I fasted on Yom Kippur; I was so hungry that I thought I was going to die, but I made it through! My hunger made me queasy, and I had to keep telling myself, "I am not going to throw up." I celebrated *Sukkot* for the first time this year, which was fun. I attended a Jewish weekend camp for adults. We had color wars and made miniature *sukkahs* (temporary huts assembled during the Jewish festival Sukkot) from graham crackers and pretzels. It was so much fun, and I met some really wonderful people. I'm taking a class about how to make your own *Shabbat*.

I know that going to classes is great from a social perspective, as I've met some truly good people while attending. I would, however, like to get more involved in a real synagogue with congregational members, which Sixth and I is not. I want to find a synagogue for *Shabbat* morning services, and it's just a matter of finding the right one. My official conversion ceremony will occur January 9, 2014, and I still need to pick a Hebrew name and make some other decisions.

I am so grateful to Rabbi Weiss, as she prepared me to be comfortable in any Jewish environment and gave me guidance about what to wear and where to sit when I attended a synagogue. She's been a great resource to me in so many aspects of Judaism and the classes I took with her. But for her, I wouldn't have my expansive and robust library of Jewish books.

I hope to go to Israel in the next year or two, perhaps as a one-year anniversary gift to myself after my conversion to Judaism. I'm a bit envious of my Jewish friends who are *Birthright Israel* (a program that sponsors a free ten-day trip to Israel for those Jews, eighteen to twenty-six, who have never visited Israel before, other than with their parents) alums!

Honestly, it's been challenging sometimes to undergo all the conversion studies and preparations as a single person; so many people do it because they are part of a couple. That was actually one of the sticking points for me early on, when one rabbi asked me, "What are you going to do if you fall in love with someone who isn't Jewish?" Some rabbis don't like to consider preparing single individuals for conversions, as they feel that there is nothing to hold them to Judaism if they are not part of an interfaith couple. Rabbi Weiss, however, fully and warmly welcomed me, just as she did her married students.

If someone were to ask me about my long journey to Judaism and all that I've learned during those many years, I think I'd respond this way: "Learn what you can and prepare yourself for surprises. The big 'take-away' is to be open to new ideas."

CHAPTER TEN

Spirituality and Science Co-Exist in a Physician's Life

*Texan Mother of Three Finds
Judaism in Midlife*

Tivona converted to Judaism because, as she herself says, "I have a Jewish soul." Neither geographic distance nor parenthood and a highly charged professional career as a physician kept her from studying with me for her conversion. Thanks to Skype and her own dedication, Tivona, a deeply spiritual physician, carved out the time needed for us to regularly meet and study together. Although she is married to someone who is not Jewish, her commitment to study and embrace Judaism was so strong that two of her three children have converted; her oldest daughter will convert sometime this spring. Tivona's deep appreciation of and awe for the natural world led her to select a Hebrew name that means "lover of nature." She has incorporated her love of nature into her own personal *Shabbat* (the Jewish Sabbath) observances during the times she cannot attend services at her synagogue in Fort Worth, Texas, due to out-of-town work commitments.

Family and Fort Worth, Texas

Tivona: I think I have a Jewish soul; I was merely the first one in my family to find it. While my mother told me that she wished she'd been Jewish, I've never talked with my father about religion. Born in 1892 in what was then Prussia and is now Poland, my maternal grandfather immigrated to the United States with my grandmother in the late 1800s. They were married in a Catholic Church, but my grandmother was fluent in Yiddish. Was it because she worked for a Jewish family and needed to communicate with them? If I could meet her, I would ask her why she knew the language. I bet that my father—whose father was Baptist—hasn't stepped into a church except for a wedding or a funeral in forty years.

My older siblings—a brother and sister—and my parents moved a lot when my father was in the Air Force; he retired when I was two years old. We lived in Fort Worth,

Texas, where I grew up and still live today.

We called ourselves Presbyterian, but only because we occasionally attended a Presbyterian church. When I was little, we went to church because we were supposed to; it didn't mean anything. Christmas was a holiday for presents, with a tree, the pie, and fudge my mother made, and watching a Christmas movie, nothing more. And Easter was merely a day to collect Easter eggs and candy.

When I was young, I didn't notice who practiced what religion. I don't think most kids pay attention to that. I was a fairly typical teenager who played field hockey in high school. I did, however, have one horribly uncomfortable and unpleasant experience during a tournament trip. Two born-again Southern Baptist girls I roomed with cornered me for hours where they pressured and challenged me, threatening me with eternal damnation, simply because I wasn't born again. They had all the right words to scare me, but I didn't believe them. It seemed a very strange way to be religious. Why would someone want to be part of such an intimidating religion that would punish you if you didn't do everything exactly right?

My best friend invited me to accompany her on a church-sponsored ski trip with her Presbyterian youth group, so I did. It was much less pressured with conversations about Bible stories' morals and ethics and some service projects. Part teen social club and part non-pressured religious group, the church group was OK, but I didn't continue with it, as it wasn't a good fit for me.

Connections with a
Jewish Community

Tivona: When I was twelve, one Jewish classmate invited everyone in our class—which was small, with only thirty-four students—to his *bar mitzvah* (the coming-of-age ritual Jewish boys experience at thirteen years old). My parents came too, and I remember thinking, "Wow, this is four hours long and he has to do all that work in another language." I was upset when a new girl came to our high school and was teased because she was Jewish. I thought that wasn't right and it bothered me, although we didn't talk about it. We're still close friends. She lives in Brooklyn, and we talk often.

Religion or Science?

Tivona: I always thought that something amazing had created this phenomenally beautiful universe. My times at Girl Scout camp might have been the genesis of it. I was amazed at how gorgeous the world was and its variety of plants, trees, animals, and sunsets. I thought that there had to be something that created it. Then, I got a biology degree and it was all about evolution, the primordial soup, the Big Bang theory. I followed the science, but I still had a deep admiration for the natural world and its beauty. Even so, I didn't think much about spirituality other than knowing something was out there. I was like Scarlett O'Hara; I'd think about it tomorrow.

I went to a very small college of only 1,200 students where I had little, if any, exposure to Judaism or even conversations about religion. Probably one-fourth of my medical school class was Jewish. I did my residency at Montefiore (in New York City), which had a strong pediatrics program. It had two Jewish hospitals; one was Orthodox and two were city hospitals. We rotated through them all. I was at the Orthodox hospital shortly before Passover began. When I went to buy a Coke one night, an employee was unloading everything from the vending machine. I didn't have any idea what he was doing; he told me he had to get everything out before Passover, but that he would bring everything back in eight days. I remember two different cafeteria lines, one with red trays and another with blue trays. That was all new to me. The only Jewish elements of the non-Orthodox Jewish hospital were *mezuzot* (plural of *mezuzah*, a prayer encased in a small decorative object placed in the doorways of Jewish homes) on the doorposts. I didn't understand anything; back then, I was a naïve little Texas girl.

I had good Jewish friends, and I began to read more and more about Judaism. I believed in some entity that had created this incredible world and in intelligent design; these things simply couldn't have happened randomly. I didn't like the idea of the Christian Trinity. It made no sense to me at all. It was like Greek mythology. I think my sister and brother and I all felt a need for some religion, as we had none when we were growing up. My brother became a very religious observant of the Bahá'í faith and my sister belongs to a nearly evangelical Presbyterian church.

With all my reading, Judaism seemed to make sense to me, especially with that mystery of my grandmother's knowledge of Yiddish.

I married my non-Jewish husband in 1991 and kicked around the idea of Judaism. In 2004, I was ready to start taking steps. Our eldest daughter was in first grade then, and I asked the moms of two of her Jewish classmates for help. One woman had a very strange reaction to my request, and the other said, "You should go to the other synagogue. We're Conservative and we're pretty intense. Why don't you check out the other synagogue?"

Through an Internet search, I found a rabbi in Florida who handled conversions, but when he called me back, I chickened out and didn't contact him again. Then, I found Rabbi Weiss who looked warm and inviting. When I talked to her, I knew she was the one. That was March of 2009; four-and-one-half years passed from the time I said, "I think I want to do this" to actually doing something about it. I had made some half-hearted attempts during that time; I'd e-mailed a synagogue in Fort Worth, but got no response.

Rabbi Weiss promised that we could do the work to fit my work schedule, so that was it for me. I so much appreciate the more personal relationship I can have with God as a Jew. When you're not Jewish, you feel like you have to go through so many levels of formality to get to God. When you're not Jewish, you have to believe this and you have to do that and if you don't believe and do those things, you'll be punished. Even today, I go out in the backyard and look up and have a conversation; I often look up at the nighttime stars and talk. It feels very comfortable, but I never thought I could do that before.

Reconciling the schism between science and religion could be hard, but for me, the concept of time in the scriptures is open-ended. A scriptural reference to "seven days" might mean seven billion years, so that's not something I worry about. The intelligent design concept makes total sense to me; there's a great guiding hand and if things evolve, a push from a creative force is responsible for that evolution.

Observing Jewish Rituals

Tivona: "Don't ask, don't tell" is my policy about religion. I know much more about Judaism than one of my husband's dearest friends who's Jewish. I started doing Jewish things and asked my family to bear with me. When I started baking bread (for *Shabbat* dinner) once a week, my family was amazed. That's because I don't normally cook at all; I usually pull pizza from the oven and press buttons on the microwave.

I began classes with Rabbi Weiss in March 2009, but I didn't get to a synagogue until August of that same year. I started going to Friday night *Kabbalat Shabbat* (reception of Shabbat) services; they're only an hour and ten minutes, so they are less intimidating and you don't have to worry about etiquette. They are an easy way to move into attending synagogue services. At the High Holidays, I did everything: I fasted and didn't wear leather. Because I'm a vegetarian, it's easy for me to follow most rules about keeping kosher. At the grocery store, I'll choose a kosher potato chip over a non-kosher chip.

I had the classic student fears on the day of my conversion—I was afraid the questions would be too difficult and that I hadn't prepared enough. I thought there'd be questions about stories in the Torah, but Rabbi Weiss reassured me that the rabbis simply wanted to know that I was truly committed to Judaism. One question, though, did surprise me; the rabbis asked me which *mitzvot* (plural of *mitzvah*, which means "commandment or obligation under Jewish law) I would try to follow that I thought would be difficult?

The *mitzvah* that cautions us against gossiping is still hard for me. In a workplace, everyone talks about everyone else, even about little things. It's so easy to be drawn into those conversations, even though I never considered myself a big gossip. People talk about each other in any social group of friends or in the workplace; even if you don't consider it gossip, it is and it's not right.

One *mitzvah* that has been easy to follow is giving to charities, something we as a family were already doing. We try to observe the rules of *Shabbat*, but sometimes it's hard to do, especially if I have to work on Sunday. If I have a deadline and really need to run to the store on a Saturday, it's a tough one.

Conversion: A Family Affair

Tivona: At the time I converted, my son was about to turn ten; when he heard about synagogue, he said, "Sure, that sounds fun." He attends a junior Torah service on Saturday morning and also religious school on Sunday. My middle child had just finished a yearlong course on comparative societies and religions at her school. Believing that Judaism "makes a lot of sense," she started attending services with me on a fairly regular basis. "This feels right; I want to be Jewish," she told me. Our oldest daughter occasionally attended services but she wasn't really interested in Judaism at that time.

Our younger daughter had an experience in school that was reminiscent of the experience I had being bullied and harassed by ultra-religious girls in high school. When she began wearing a Star of David necklace, some kids at school started teasing her by saying, "Why are you wearing that necklace? You're not Jewish."

Although she explained that her mother was Jewish and that she felt Jewish, some evangelical Christian girls said, "You'll be damned if you do this . . . you can't do it." She was ready, I think, to convert until those girls got to her. She loves the rituals of the *Shabbat* blessings, with the candles and the *challah* (a sweet, braided bread often served at *Shabbat* dinners and special holiday meals). She decided that she's not ready to commit to anything, even though she doesn't believe what the girls said to her.

When my oldest daughter told me that she wanted to convert, I was surprised, given her initial disinterest. But I had given both my daughters many of the materials I was reading and talked with them about what I was learning. She had started attending services more often. As she loves to sing, she was picking up the Hebrew so

quickly in singing songs that I think she learned Hebrew more quickly than I did! So, my conversion led to
the conversions about a year later of my oldest daughter
and my son; they had their conversion ceremonies in
January 2013. Now, my middle daughter has considered
undergoing her own conversion ceremony in Washington, DC. Now dating a Jewish boy, she is impressed by
the friendly and positive attitude of people she meets
at our synagogue. It's different, she explained, than the
glum, serious, and depressed attitudes and behaviors
she's witnessed among churchgoing friends. I shared my
perspective on those differences with her—I believe it's
the difference between focusing on l'chaim (a celebratory
toast that means "to life") and on worrying about salva-
tion and heaven.

Before I had my conversion, I would go to services
two Saturdays every month. I'd stay and have lunch at
the *oneg Shabbat* (light lunch or other refreshments
served after Saturday morning services) with a wonderful
group of women. I was very involved in the synagogue
and sometimes attended Friday night services, as well.
My son joked that, now that he's Jewish, he doesn't get
a break: "I enjoy it, but I never get to sleep in . . . there's
Friday nights and Saturday mornings and then Sunday
school."

I was astonished when our rabbi recounted the conversation she and my son, then not yet ten, had during
Sukkot. During religious school, the children were
discussing which seven individuals they would invite
into their *sukkahs* (temporary huts assembled during

the Jewish festival Sukkot). Although the children initially identified sports figures and pop singers, they were encouraged to think more seriously about the "invited guests." My son said that he would invite Hitler. Taking a breath and pausing for a moment, the rabbi then asked him why. My son responded, "I want to show him that I'm still here. We're all still here." Explaining that no one had ever expressed that idea to him, he told me, "Even if there was a third or fourth or fifth Holocaust, we, the Jews, would still be here; nothing people could to do to us would affect us because God protects us."

It's funny, when I look now at photographs of the synagogue's confirmation classes from past years, I say, "I know that person, I know that person . . . ." I had no idea they were Jewish. There were so many people who I grew up with who belonged to one of the two synagogues in Fort Worth; I just never knew they were Jewish.

Since my conversion, I have a new job that requires me to be out of town for several days at a time. In my old position, I would sometimes work two or three shifts in a row. With that, I might not see the kids for several days at a time, between their school and my work schedules. With this new position, I'm gone for several days and then home for several days, so I see them more. I'm very disappointed with the outcome of my efforts to connect with the synagogue in that new location; it's a combined Reform and Conservative congregation. I e-mailed the synagogue asking about the *siddur* (prayer book) it uses, and I heard nothing. I e-mailed again with some specific questions, and heard nothing. In my third e-mail,

I wrote, "I'm an active member of a synagogue in Fort Worth; I am not a kook. They will vouch for me; I'm a legitimate Jewish woman looking for a synagogue." I also included contact names and numbers for them to verify my interest and legitimacy, but they never acknowledged that e-mail. Even so, I went there one *Shabbat* morning, and two services were being held. The Conservative service had more Hebrew than the Reform one, but they used a *siddur* I didn't know; its translations of the Hebrew prayers were just ridiculous. It felt like we were reading from a middle school textbook, and the rabbi was very uninspiring. They started the service without having a *minyan* (the ten adults needed under Jewish law to hold a service), and the rabbi didn't read directly from the Torah; he read from some photocopied pages instead. At my Conservative synagogue in Fort Worth, something touches me at every service—whether it's a prayer or a song or something that the rabbi said—but here, nothing, nothing got through to me. The place wasn't Jewish enough for me; I've come a long way.

So, now that I spend half my time in that city, before sunset on Friday nights, I go to the beach and sing along to a tape of songs from the *Kabbalat Shabbat* (reception of Shabbat) service from the Fort Worth synagogue. And, on holidays, I can watch a service on my laptop. When I'm out of town, I "make do." I'm disappointed that it didn't work out with the only synagogue here, but I still attend services in Fort Worth. I love the synagogue there; it's amazingly welcoming and helpful.

I haven't been to Israel yet, but I hope to go. It's an

amazing place for Jewish history. Israel is an incredibly modern, vibrant country, but many Americans think it's just a desert country with a couple of cities. People have no idea that it developed texting and smart phones and pioneered so many medical techniques to address mass disasters. There are always so many negative headlines about Israel with respect to the Palestinians. I've thought about making *aliyah* (moving to Israel), but I think I'm so needed here for my family and my work. I don't know if I'd ever live there permanently.

I'm exactly where I should be with my Judaism. It took me a long time, but I wouldn't have been ready earlier. I needed to be in a secure position before I could experience the conversion. I'm not worried about what anyone else feels or thinks; I'm doing this for me. My Hebrew name, Tivona, means "lover of nature." When I sit in nature and go on backpacking trips and look at Bryce Canyon, I recognize the privilege it is to live in this amazing place.

GLOSSARY

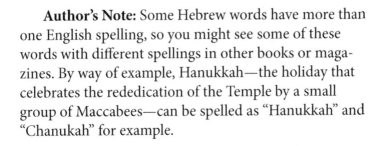

Author's Note: Some Hebrew words have more than one English spelling, so you might see some of these words with different spellings in other books or magazines. By way of example, Hanukkah—the holiday that celebrates the rededication of the Temple by a small group of Maccabees—can be spelled as "Hanukkah" and "Chanukah" for example.

Aliyah: Ascent or the act of "going up." It generally refers to moving to Israel with the intention of living there permanently (as used in this book). It also means being called up to the Torah, in order to bless the reading of the Torah.

Bar Mitzvah: The coming-of-age ritual Jewish boys experience at thirteen years old; literally, "son of commandment."

Bat Mitzvah: The coming-of-age ritual Jewish girls experience at twelve or thirteen years old; literally, "daughter of commandment."

Beit Din: Rabbinic court of Jewish laws

Beshert: Meant to be, often used in the context of finding one's beloved partner.

Bimah: Platform or podium in a synagogue.

Birthright Israel: A program that sponsors a free ten-day trip to Israel for those Jews, eighteen to twenty-six, who have never visited Israel before, other than with their parents

B'nei Mitzvah: More than one bar mitzvah or more than one bar mitzvah and bat mitzvah

B'not Mitzvah: The plural of bat mitzvah

Bubbie: Yiddish for grandmother

Chabad: A Jewish outreach organization unaffiliated with the Reform, Conservative, or Orthodox movements

Challah: A sweet, braided bread often served at Shabbat dinners and special holiday meals

Haroset: Mixture of apples and wine served during the Passover Seder; sometimes spelled as "charoset"

Hamantashen: A triangular-shaped pastry, filled with fruit preserves or poppy seed filing, served during Purim, a festive Jewish holiday

Havdalah: The ceremony that signifies the end of Shabbat, after three stars can be seen in the Saturday evening sky

Hazzan: A cantor; an individual trained in Jewish music and liturgy

Hekshered: Approved as kosher

Hillel: A college-based Jewish program

Hineni: Part of a prayer that means, "Here I am, God"

Judaica: Jewlery, art, textiles, etc. from Israel

Kabbalat Shabbat: Reception of the Shabbat; designates the authorization of the Shabbat in general. It is part of Friday evening service, which precedes the regular evening service and welcomes the Shabbat

Kashered: The process of making a space kosher

Kavanah: Holy intention

Kippah: A head covering that many Jewish men and some Jewish women wear

Kippot: Head covering

L'chaim: A celebratory toast that means "to life"

Menorah: Candlestick holder used in Jewish worship that holds seven candles

Mezuzah: A prayer scroll in a small, decorative fixture affixed to the doorways of Jewish homes

Mezuzot: The plural of mezuzah

Mikveh: A bath used for the purpose of ritual immersion. The word "mikveh," as used in the Hebrew Bible, literally means a collection—generally a collection of water. The mikveh can be used as part of con-

version ceremonies, before weddings, and to adhere
to laws of family purity.

Minyan: The ten adults needed under Jewish law to hold
a service

Mitzvah: Commandment or obligation under Jewish law

Mitzvot: Plural of mitzvah

Mufti: A religious Sunni leader with more authority than
a Sheikh

Oneg Shabbat: Light lunch or other refreshments served
after Saturday morning services

Shabbat: The Jewish Sabbath

Seder: The Passover ritual meal to observe the liberation
of the Jews after being exiled from Egypt and wandering in the desert for 40 years. Seder means "order"
as there is a precise order of the readings that are
recited before and after the holiday meal.

Shalom Bay'yit: A peaceful Jewish home; Shalom means
peace and bay'yit means home.

Sheikh: Religious leader equivalant to a priest who is
legally allowed to perform marriages

Shomer Shabbas: Honoring the commandment to spend
Shabbat in prayer, study, and communal Jewish life,
rather than spending money, driving, or engaging in
other commercial activities

Siddur: Prayer book

Shoah: The Holocaust perpetrated by the Nazis during World War II that led to the murders of six million Jews

Shuls: Synagogues

Sukkahs Temporary hut assembled during the Jewish festival Sukkot

Tallitot: Prayer shawls

Tikkun Olam: Healing or repairing the world through good acts or good deeds

Tzedakah: To perform acts of charity or donate money

Zayde: Yiddish for grandfather

ABOUT THE AUTHORS

Rabbi Bernice Kimel Weiss is the founder and director of the Washington Institute for Conversion and the Study of Judaism, located in Washington, DC. Rabbi Weiss earned a BS from the University of Pittsburgh and a MA from George Washington University. Upon graduating from the Academy for Jewish Religion in 1989, she entered the rabbinate. Rabbi Weiss received the prestigious Melton Senior Educators Fellowship for Jewish Education in the Diaspora and spent 1995 and 1996 at Hebrew University in Jerusalem. Her first book, Converting to Judaism: Choosing to Be Chosen; Personal Stories was published by Simcha Press in 2000. She is a member of the United Jewish Communities Rabbinic Cabinet and the Washington Board of Rabbis.

Nancy Kirsch, a former corporate lobbyist and attorney, was most recently the editor of The Jewish Voice, the Jewish newspaper of record for Rhode Island, for several years. Now a freelance writer for a wide array of newspapers and magazines, she has earned several awards for her writing. Raised in Indianapolis, Indiana, she lives in Providence, Rhode Island, with her family.

Printed in Great Britain
by Amazon

20188618R00092